HOW TO BECOME A WEDDING PLANNER

How to Become a Wedding Planner

ZUBAIR ABDUL WAHEED

Edited by Neha Mishra

First Printing, 2025

CONTENTS

DEDICATION

To my beloved wife, **Shaistha Hasan**, and my wonderful children, **Ruhan Zubair** and **Inara Zubair**, you are my constant source of strength and inspiration.

To my parents, **HG Abdul Waheed** and **Syeda Seema Zahra**, for your unwavering love, values, and blessings.

A special tribute to my **Ammijaan (Granny)**, whose belief in me lit the first spark of my journey in this industry. Without her, it would never have begun.

And to **Mama Shakeel Adeeb**, thank you for your support and encouragement when it mattered most.

To my dear siblings, **Asim AH, Faisal AH,** and **Haniya Fathima**, thank you for your love and presence in my life.

To my respected father-in-law, **Dr. ZML Hasan**, and my gracious mother-in-law, **Ayesha Siddika**, your warmth and support have meant the world to me. Each one of you is woven into the fabric of this journey.

Last but not least, this book is dedicated to the **entire wedding fraternity.**

With all my heart, I thank you.

| 1 |

Introduction

Your Journey in Event Management Starts Here!

Imagine being 21 years old and earning lakhs every month. Sounds unreal, right?

That's exactly where I found myself, not because of luck, but because of the lessons I learned, the risks I took, and the passion I poured into my work. My journey in event management was less about organizing events & more about understanding people, solving problems, and creating unforgettable experiences. And now, I want to share those lessons with you, so you can build your own success story.

Today, I stand having led 7,000+ events worldwide. That includes weddings in Bahrain, Hong Kong, Macau, and many other countries. But before all of this, I was just like you...starting out, unsure of where my path would lead. My journey began during college, where I stumbled into the world of fashion shows and choreography. Little did I know that this accidental entry would shape the rest of my career.

Back then, I was just a fitness enthusiast, working out regularly and trying to stay fit. One of my seniors noticed me and said, "Why don't you join the fashion team? Just come and check it out." I thought, "Okay, fine, I'll give it a try." That year, I joined the team, and the next year, the college asked me to handle the entire event myself.

At that time, I was also training at Shiamak Davar's dance academy. I had been there for about two years, and I thought, "Why not incorporate what I'm learning into the fashion show?" So, I choreographed the entire event, and we came in second place. The first place went to Mount Carmel College because they had professional models, so we didn't stand a chance. But the following year, we got the runner-up position again, and I was awarded Best Choreographer.

One of the judges saw my work and asked if I'd like to choreograph for his shows. He said, "What you're doing is unique, and people want to try it in our shows." I agreed and did a couple of shows for him, but I was never properly credited. My hard work was left unrecognized. It was frustrating, but it taught me the importance of standing up for myself and owning my contributions.

From there, I started coordinating models and organizing fashion shows. Around that time, a friend introduced me to a brand called Welkins. The client wanted to launch his brand, and I negotiated a deal with the owner of an open-air lounge. We organized the event, and the turnout exceeded all expectations. The client expected 100–150 people, but more than a thousand people showed up. It became the biggest party of the month.

That success opened doors to more opportunities. I started partnering with clubs and cafes, introducing innovative concepts like daytime hookah services. I suggested they run "50% off" offers, which increased footfall significantly. At one point, I had six cafes running simultaneously, each generating between Rupees 35,000 and Rupees 85,000 daily. The business was booming, and I was just a teenager at the time.

But the commercial event space came with its own challenges. As I gained recognition, influential people started asking for free passes. They were oblivious to the fact that everything came with a cost. The commercial scene started to deteriorate, so I decided it wasn't worth continuing. No matter how good the artist or event, if you're not making money, what's the point?

That's when I shifted my focus to weddings. Weddings allowed me to connect with clients on a personal level and bring their visions to life. My approach to weddings is deeply personal. I become like a family member to my clients, ensuring every detail reflects their dreams. This personal touch has helped me build a reputation and a loyal clientele.

One of my proudest achievements was creating a two-floor stage, where 30 people could stand on the first floor and another 60 people could stand below for family photos. I was one of the first in South India to do this, and that stage is still in demand today.

Over the years, I've organized some of the largest-scale events in the country, including the VH1 10th Anniversary New Year's Bash, which saw nearly 9,000 attendees. I've also learned the art of securing sponsorships, managing budgets, and delivering events that leave a lasting impression.

But here's the thing: you don't have to go through the same struggles I did. This book is your guide to avoiding the pitfalls and embracing the opportunities in event management. Whether you're just starting out or looking to refine your skills, you'll find practical insights, checklists, and strategies to help you succeed.

You'll learn how to:

- Innovate and think outside the box to create unique experiences.
- Build strong relationships with clients, vendors, and teams.
- Manage budgets and sponsorships effectively to ensure profitability.
- Adapt to challenges and turn them into opportunities.
- Deliver events that leave a lasting impact.

My journey wasn't easy, but it was worth it. And now, I want to make your journey a little easier. Whether you dream of organizing grand weddings, corporate events, or innovative concepts like daytime hookah services, this book will give you the tools and confidence to make it happen.

So, are you ready to take the first step? Let's dive in and start building your success story in event management.

MODULE 1

UNDERSTANDING THE ROLE OF A WEDDING PLANNER

"A wedding planner turns dreams into plans and plans into memories."-**Unknown**

| 2 |

Definition and Scope of a Wedding Planner

You're not planning an event. You're making someone's dream come true.

Weddings, in particular, are very challenging because they are so detail-oriented. With so many people involved, every detail makes a difference. Every function matters, and emotions play a huge role. It's a once-in-a-lifetime event for someone. You can't afford to miss anything.

For me, it's always about creating something new. I love building and creating things. Even when I watch behind-the-scenes (BTS) videos of events, I get curious and want to learn how things are done. That curiosity is what drove me to start learning and eventually led me into weddings and corporate events.

You might assume that planning an event is just about logistics. More so, a wedding planner's job is to make sure the family feels at ease and doesn't have to worry about the wedding. My goal is to build trust with the family, so they feel confident handing over their dream to me. In simple terms, it's about executing someone else's dream.

There have been instances where brides have asked for things that were difficult to execute, especially when the venue didn't support their vision.

In one case, the bride wanted a varmala shot with a clear sky, but the venue didn't allow it. So, we did the varmala on the rooftop of a building with a clear sky. We got the shot, and the video turned out amazing. The bride was thrilled because we made her vision come true in a creative way. Nobody had anticipated executing something like this.

Consultation

The most important thing is to read the client and understand their brief completely. You need to know what they have in mind, their ideas, and their expectations. Once you have that, you can start building on it.

Some people say you should never ask a client about their budget, but I disagree. I always try to understand the client's budget first. If their ideas exceed the budget, I inform them and suggest alternatives.

They think it's about making more money than the client is willing to spend. But I believe in being transparent. I've seen families take loans to fulfill the bride or groom's demands, and I'm certain, just like me, you don't want that to happen.

Vendor Coordination

When you're starting out, always get reviews of the vendor before working with them. Even the best vendors can have bad days, but that doesn't define them. If a vendor has done 99 good events and one bad one, that one event shouldn't overshadow their reputation.

Over the years, I've remained loyal to certain vendors because of the quality of their work and the trust we've built. They understand my expectations, and I don't have to micromanage them.

Building relationships with vendors is crucial. It takes time, but trust is key. Even if you're new, don't show the vendor that you don't know things. Always ask questions and learn from them.

Yes, there will be times when vendors don't show up. Once, we called a vendor a day earlier, but they didn't arrive. Luckily, we had a backup plan and called a friend in the industry who came in at midnight and set everything up for the morning event.

Venue Selection

It depends on the client's preferences and budget. Some clients want an outdoor venue, like a poolside or beachside location. Others prefer indoor venues. The key is to match the venue with the client's vision.

Design

You can either hire a designer or take on the role yourself. If you're designing the wedding, you need to understand the bride and groom's likes and dislikes, as well as their family's traditions. For example, some Hindu families don't want marigold flowers in their wedding, while Marwari families avoid black in their decor.

I always try to understand the client's perspective and give them options. For example, in a recent meeting, we discussed a peacock theme for the bride's entry. The groom's sister suggested adding peacock sounds along the pathway, but I felt it didn't suit the theme. However, I didn't impose my opinion. I let them decide because their happiness is what matters.

Timeline Creation

Planning is 80% of the wedding, and execution is 20%. Clear communication between vendors, planners, and clients is crucial. If the client says the event starts at 5 PM, the vendor should be ready by 3 PM. That two-hour buffer is essential for handling any last-minute issues.

For instance, if the venue is available a day before the event, use that time to set up and avoid last-minute stress. Detailing plays a huge role in decor and execution. If an artist is performing, they should have time to rehearse on stage beforehand. This ensures a smooth performance and a great experience for everyone.

Logistics

I believe that hiring the right vendor for logistics makes everything easier. You don't need to stress over every detail because once you dive too deep into logistics, other aspects of the event start to suffer. Always have a dedicated team and a manager overseeing logistics. Let the professionals handle it while you focus on the bigger picture.

Logistics is a 24-hour job because you never know when vendors or guests will arrive — some guests come at night, some guest arrive during the day. If you get too involved in logistics, your work on the event itself will suffer. You need a separate team for logistics that isn't tied to your decor, sound, lighting, or fabrication teams. Their sole focus should be logistics.

Day of Coordination

As a wedding planner, you need to have assigned managers for every department like decor, catering, sound, lighting, etc. Your job is to take feedback from these managers, walk around, and address any issues that arise. If there's a problem, you either fix it or find a way to work around it.

Imagine you've done all the 3D designs, taken measurements, and planned the layout. And on the setup day, the hotel decides last minute to install a chandelier in the middle of your LED wall setup. What do you do? Do you resize the LED wall, move the stage, or change the layout? These decisions need to be made quickly, and the wedding planner must be free to handle them.

If you get too deep into every department, you'll lose focus. A good wedding is the result of a strong team, not just the wedding planner.

Post Wedding Tasks

It's time to finalize payments and gather feedback. My philosophy has always been to prioritize paying the laborers first. They work incredibly hard to make the event happen, and their payment should come before anything else. After that, you can start clearing payments with vendors.

Feedback should come from the family itself. But here's something many planners don't realize: you need to be friendly with every guest. Get to know them because you never know who might provide valuable feedback or become a future client.

Let's Talk Money

It's also important to align with the client on payment schedules. My suggestion is to always collect your money before the event. For clients you trust, it's okay to leave a small percentage for later. But for clients you're unsure about, make sure you collect the full payment before the event.

A common structure is 50% upfront, 30% during the wedding, and 20% after the event. But as clients started becoming more unpredictable, we shifted to 80% before the wedding and 20% during. Some planners even take 100% upfront, but that's a rare case.

I've had incidents where we provided complete 3D designs, presentations, and executed everything perfectly, only for the client to later claim they weren't satisfied. In one case, a client tried to downplay our work, but I had all the documentation to prove we delivered exactly what was promised.

As long as you're in business, incidents like this will happen. Later in this book, I'll prepare you to handle these tricky situations in your favour.

| 3 |

Skills & Qualities of a Successful Wedding Planner

What's the one thing that will make your events stand out in the long run Well, it's not what you think.

Over the years, I've witnessed massive changes, from the rise of digital to the demand for more personalized, immersive experiences. The pace of evolution is only speeding up.

As I look ahead, one question keeps surfacing: What skills will be essential for event professionals to survive and thrive in the next five years? Here's what I've come to believe.

Organizational Skills

Always prepare yourself before meeting a client. Do your homework and understand who the client is. Never sell something the client doesn't need. Clients aren't fools, and trying to upsell unnecessarily can ruin your reputation.

Communication

Communication is key. Always have a single point of contact in the family. During the wedding, there will be 20–30 people trying to make changes to plans that have been in place for months. The bride, groom, and family members will all have opinions, and some may even try to disrupt things out of jealousy.

To avoid chaos, establish that you'll only take instructions from one person. If anyone else has concerns, they should go through that person. This system ensures that only necessary changes are made, and unnecessary requests are filtered out.

Problem-Solving

Problem-solving is crucial. Always have a backup plan and be ready to think on your feet. For example, if a vendor doesn't show up, you need to have contacts who can step in at the last minute.

The most important thing is to stay calm and focused. If you panic, the entire team will feel it, and the event will suffer.

Clear communication with the client and vendors is crucial, especially during chaos. When the atmosphere is positive, even in the midst of chaos, opportunities to solve problems arise.

This is very important to understand. When the atmosphere is positive, you feel good, right? When you approach chaos with a positive mindset, your brain starts thinking of ways to tackle the situation calmly and effectively.

Suddenly, ideas start flowing, and solutions present themselves. But if you're panicking, shouting, or stressing, you won't be able to think clearly.

Chaos can be an opportunity. You can either use it to create something great or learn from it to ensure it doesn't happen again.

Creativity

In the span of your career, whether you're an event planner, businessman, or entrepreneur, you need to dedicate at least 30 minutes every day to research and innovation in your field. This is very, very important.

The first thing you should do in the morning is dedicate 30 minutes to improving your skills. Whether it's reading, researching, or learning something new. This daily practice will help you stay ahead in the industry.

If you don't keep enhancing your skills, you'll fall behind. When a client mentions something they've seen elsewhere, and if you've already researched it, you can confidently discuss it with them. It gives the client comfort knowing you're knowledgeable.

And there's no harm in admitting when you don't know something. You can always say, "I don't know about this, but I'll find out and get back to you." Honesty builds trust.

Time Management

Time management is critical. You need to stay organized and prioritize tasks to ensure everything runs smoothly.

One of the most effective strategies I've used is the "two-hour rule". What's the two hour rule? Dedicate the first two hours of your day to the most important tasks. This is when your mind is fresh, and you can tackle complex challenges without distractions. Also, always build in buffer time for unexpected delays. For example, if a vendor says they'll arrive by 3 PM, plan for them to arrive by 2 PM. This way, you're prepared for any last-minute changes.

Negotiation

Negotiation should always be fair. Don't go for the cheapest option because cheap things aren't always good.

Get three quotes, and you'll see the difference. But remember, different vendors offer different prices based on the quality of their services. For example, if one vendor offers RCF sound systems for Rupees 14,000 and another offers JBL for Rupees 10,000, neither is wrong. RCF is better than JBL, but if another vendor offers D&B

sound systems for Rupees 30,000, they're also not wrong because the quality is superior.

You need to understand the event's requirements. For a small event, JBL might suffice, but for a high-profile event with a celebrity performer who demands D&B, you'll need to invest in the best.

When it comes to vendor contracts, always ensure the contract clearly states the agreed terms and rates. Both parties should stick to what's been discussed.

Empathy and Patience

Yes, clients are often emotional during the wedding planning process. It's important to be empathetic and patient. However, make sure to set boundaries and finish all necessary discussions before the event starts.

Special Note For Event Planners

Not every event day goes as planned.

For me, it's never about the months of preparation or the detailed agenda. Your thorough preparations can save you from making mistakes, but your mistakes will offer lifelong lessons. It's about those unexpected moments that catch you off guard.

Like the time it rained during an outdoor gala, and we ended up standing in water while trying to save decorations. Or the time a key speaker missed their flight, and we had to rewrite the entire schedule. In those moments, it feels like everything is falling apart. But here's what I've learned: chaos doesn't win. Those are the moments when my team steps up in ways I never imagined.

Someone grabs the mic to calm the crowd. Another comes up with a solution no one thought of. These aren't things you plan for but they happen because of trust, determination, and the belief that giving up is not an option. Over the years, I've realized that chaos is just part of events.

We once experienced a blackout during a live event. Even a 10-second blackout can feel like forever when everything comes to a standstill. A brief power outage might seem minor, but in those 10 seconds, when the music cut out, the lights faded...the energy of the room wavered.

Moments like these remind us how crucial it is to expect the unexpected.

That's why I always go the extra mile to ensure events run seamlessly, **no matter what**.

Here's how you should plan for unforeseen circumstances:

-**Backup Generators:** We never rely solely on the venue's power. Our team ensures every event is powered to perfection with reliable external generators.

-**Contingency Planning:** When external generators aren't an option, we implement quick and efficient solutions to maximize the venue's existing power.

Uninterrupted Experiences: Every plan we make centers around ensuring nothing interrupts the special moments someone has dreamed of.

We prepare for it with backup plans, contingency teams, and even a bit of humor to keep spirits up. But what really gets us through is knowing we'll figure it out together. No matter what happens, we'll adapt, deliver, and make it work.

Event days are never perfect, and they don't need to be. They remind us how strong and resourceful we truly are. So, when you're facing your own "event day," whether at work or in life, remember: you've got this. Trust yourself, trust your team, and keep going.

| 4 |

Wedding Planners vs Coordinators vs Designers

Let me break down something crucial that most people get confused about. When I first started in this industry, even I didn't fully understand the distinct roles everyone plays. Trust me, knowing this will save you a lot of headaches and help you position yourself correctly in the market.

Wedding Planners

A wedding planner is essentially the CEO of the entire wedding. We're the ones who handle everything from day one until the last guest leaves the venue. I remember when I took on my first full wedding planning job it was overwhelming because I was responsible for literally everything.

The thing about being a wedding planner is that you're constantly juggling multiple responsibilities:

- Creating and managing the entire budget (and trust me, this alone can be a nightmare.)
- Finding and negotiating with every vendor, from caterers to photographers
- Building timelines that account for every minute of the event

- Coordinating logistics like guest transportation and accommodations
- Handling any family drama that inevitably comes up (and there's always drama!)

What makes wedding planning so challenging is that you're with the family from the very beginning. You become so deeply involved in their lives that by the end, you're practically a family member except you don't get invited to the next Diwali gathering until something needs planning.

Wedding Coordinators

Now, wedding coordinators have a more focused role. Think of them as the stage managers who come in during the final act. They're not involved in the early planning phases but are crucial for execution.

I once had a client who had planned everything herself but hired me just for coordination during the final month. She had spreadsheets for everything vendor contacts, payments, timelines. But what she didn't realize was how chaotic the actual wedding day would be. When the flower vendor arrived two hours late and the bride was having a meltdown, she understood why a coordinator was essential.

Wedding coordinators typically:

- Step in about 4-6 weeks before the wedding
- Review all vendor contracts to ensure everything is in order
- Create detailed day-of timelines
- Manage the rehearsal
- Solve any last-minute problems during the event

The beauty of being a coordinator is that you get to be the hero without the months of planning stress. You walk in fresh when everyone else is exhausted, and you save the day. But also, the challenge is that you're expected to understand 6 months of planning in 60 minutes.

Wedding Designers

Wedding designers are the artists of the wedding world. These are the people who transform an ordinary space into something magical. I've worked with some phenomenal designers who could walk into an empty hall and envision exactly how to transform it into a breathtaking wonderland.

A good designer is obsessed with:

- Creating a cohesive theme and aesthetic
- Selecting color palettes that reflect the couple's personality
- Choosing florals, lighting, and decor elements
- Designing the spatial layout for maximum impact

I once worked with a bride who dreamed of making a grand entrance on a mirror floor, capturing the perfect reflections for her wedding photographs. The designer crafted a stunning mirrored aisle that shimmered with candles and floral arrangements, creating a surreal, almost fairytale-like effect. Every step she took felt like walking on a dream. That's the magic a good designer brings.

The Regional Differences

Let me tell you something interesting I've observed over the years. The wedding industry works very differently depending on where you are in India.

From my experience, there's a noticeable difference between wedding planners in the South, North, and West. In the North and West, the system is more hierarchical. Wedding planners have coordinators within their own teams, and those coordinators oversee designers. The designer's team includes production houses, floral designers, and other specialized roles. At the top of this hierarchy is the wedding planner.

But in Bangalore, it's simpler. You typically have a wedding planner and a decorator. That's it. In the North, budgets are much larger. A wedding that costs Rupees 30 lakhs in Bangalore might cost Rupees 3–4 crores in the North. The wedding planner's fee alone can be Rupees 25–30 lakhs, whereas in Bangalore, the planner and decorator together might charge Rupees 30 lakhs for the entire wedding.

There are some high-budget weddings in Bangalore, but they're rare, maybe 2% of the clientele. These weddings can go up to Rupees 50–80 lakhs, but very few planners in the South can handle that scale. In the North, however, handling such weddings is more common. However, what you can see in both North & South is some decorators use the same materials and textiles across multiple weddings. For example, they'll set up trusses and tents with fabric in one wedding and reuse them in another. In the North, we use materials only once.

Finding Your Place

If you're reading this book because you want to enter the wedding industry, you need to decide which of these roles best suits your skills and interests.

Are you detail-oriented and great at managing logistics? Maybe being a wedding planner or coordinator is your calling.

Are you creative and have an eye for aesthetics? Then wedding design might be your path.

Or maybe, like me, you want to do it all. That's possible too, but remember that it takes years to master each aspect.

Whatever you choose, understand that weddings are emotional events for families. You're not just planning an event; you're creating memories that will last a lifetime. That responsibility should never be taken lightly.

In the next section, I'll walk you through how to conduct that crucial first meeting with clients because how you start determines how the rest of the planning process will go.

MODULE 2

THE WEDDING PLANNING PROCESS (INITIAL CONSULTATION)

"A good wedding planner listens to your heart and brings it to life."-**Unknown**

| 5 |

How to Conduct Initial Consultation with Clients

The key to success is reading the client correctly. When you show them exactly what's in their mind, that's when you win. Let me share a story of how we stole the wedding of a family who was fixated on another Mumbai-based event planner for their Big Day.

I got a call from a college friend whose brother's wedding I had planned. He referred me to his father's sister's daughter's wedding. The client was a typical Marwari businessman who wanted to show off. He told me, "I've hired a caterer for 250 dishes. I know no guest will eat all 250 dishes, but I want to showcase that I can afford it."

Before me, he had already met a Mumbai planner and a Bangalore planner. For him, hiring a Mumbai planner was a status symbol. It showed he could afford to fly someone in for the wedding.

During our meeting, I tried to connect with him, but he wasn't interested in hearing my perspective. My friend and I, who had traveled with me, suggested we meet the bride.

We arranged to meet her at one of the local shops. I sat her down and asked, "What's on your mind? What do you want for your wedding?" I wanted to understand her taste and vision. I pulled out my phone and dived into our previous works that matched her taste. Based on her answers, I showed her examples of our work that matched her preferences, right from my phone (not a laptop).

When I showed her a grand entry concept inspired by a Lebanese wedding planned by us — where the bride's childhood story was projected with graphics, and she made a dramatic entrance with her father — she loved it. After the meeting, the family asked us to prepare a presentation.

My team and I worked on an 85–87 pager presentation tailored to the bride's vision. A few days later, we traveled to Mysore to present it. The father was still inclined toward the Mumbai planner, but the mother liked our presentation. The Mumbai planner had ignored the bride's preferences, focusing only on what the father wanted. I did the opposite. I listened to the bride and designed the wedding around her vision.

That wasn't all. During the discussion, I had a clever trick up my sleeve. I brought a Marwari team member with me but instructed him to only speak in Hindi, not Marwari. This helped me understand if the family was discussing anything privately.

Then suddenly an idea clicked. This was the ultimate deal maker. I pitched an idea to the mother: "We'll hire a lyricist to compose a song about your family's history. We'll create a wedding anthem and use it in videos, entries, and other parts of the wedding. We can even shoot a documentary-style video." And just when you would have thought that this was enough, I went ahead and added that we could capture their family's love, history, and togetherness in this song. The mother was moved to tears.

She went inside, spoke to the father and daughter, and walked back into the room with a bag full of cash. She said, "Only you will handle this wedding. No one else."

We had read the bride perfectly and won over the mother. The catch is, we charged 20% more than the Mumbai planner, and yet this was a win-win for everyone.

Unfortunately, COVID hit, and the grand wedding with Benny Dayal and Ranvijay hosting had to be scaled down. But the family still has the budget saved for their younger daughter's wedding, which might happen next year. We may finally see Benny Dayal at this wedding. That's how important it is to read the client. If you can't connect with one person, find someone else in the family who can advocate for you.

It's like American X-Factor... you need two out of three votes. Sometimes, the bride may not want you, but the parents do. In such cases, we show the value we bring, like saving money or adding unique touches. Once we start working with the bride, we win her over by understanding her wishes and making those come true.

Conducting Initial Consultation with Clients:

Preparation: The Groundwork for Success

I always say planning is 80% of the wedding, and that starts with your very first interaction. Over the years, I've learned that the initial consultation sets the tone for the entire planning journey. It's not just about selling your services; it's about building a connection that will last through one of the most important days of your client's life.

Before you even meet your potential clients, the real work begins.

• **Review any preliminary information provided by the clients.**

Don't just skim through the WhatsApp messages or emails they've sent you. Read between the lines. If a bride mentions she loves mogra flowers but her wedding is in a season when they're not easily available, make a note to discuss alternatives. If the groom says he wants to make an entry in the wedding on a bullet, take note. We've literally made that happen for a groom.

• **Prepare a list of questions and topics to cover during the meeting.**

Your questions should go beyond the basics. Yes, you need to know the *muhurat*, venue preferences, and *baraat* count. But you also need to ask about their story: how they met, what makes their relationship special, and what moments they want to highlight at their wedding. These details will help you create a truly personalized experience.

• Bring materials like portfolios, brochures, and a sample contract.

Visual aids make a huge difference. I've seen couples' and their parents' eyes light up when they see photos of *Mandaps* and stage setups I've designed that align with their vision. But remember, don't overwhelm them with options. Curate your portfolio based on their preferences and cultural background.

Greeting and Introduction: Making That First Impression Count

• Start with a warm and friendly greeting.

Seems obvious, right? But you'd be surprised how many planners jump straight into business mode. Remember, this couple is entrusting you with one of the most important days of their lives. A genuine smile and a firm handshake (or a warm virtual greeting) goes a long way.

• Introduce yourself and provide a brief overview of your experience and services.

This is your chance to shine, but keep it brief and relevant. If you're meeting a family planning a destination wedding in Udaipur, highlight your experience in Rajasthani weddings. If they're looking for something intimate, talk about the small, meaningful ceremonies you've planned while still maintaining traditional elements.

Establishing Rapport: Building the Foundation of Trust

• Engage in small talk to make clients comfortable.

But here's the thing, it shouldn't feel like small talk. Be genuinely interested in them as people, not just as clients. Maybe they mentioned they just moved back from abroad, or perhaps one of them is from a different state. These conversations build a personal connection that will serve you well throughout the planning process.

• Show genuine interest in their story and vision.

We once were working with a bride who was initially very guarded during our first meeting. We were finalized as wedding planners by her parents. When I asked about her family traditions and what elements were most important to both families, her entire demeanor changed. She opened up, sharing beautiful stories about her grandmother's jewelry that she wanted to incorporate into her bridal look. That conversation gave me insights into their values and priorities that no questionnaire could have captured.

Outline the Meeting: Setting Clear Expectations

• Explain the purpose of the meeting and what you aim to accomplish.

This sets a professional tone and shows that you value their time. I usually say something like, "Today, I'd like to understand your vision for your wedding, discuss your budget and timeline, and see if we're a good fit. I want to learn about your family traditions and how we can honor them while creating a beautiful celebration."

• Mention the key points you'll cover: budget, vision, timeline, and expectations.

Don't shy away from the budget conversation. Remember what I said earlier? I always try to understand the client's budget first. If their ideas exceed the budget, I inform them and suggest alternatives. For instance, if they want an elaborate *sangeet* setup but have budget constraints, I might suggest combining the *mehendi* and *sangeet* functions to maximize resources. This transparency builds trust from the very beginning.

Listening and Note-Taking: The Most Underrated Skills

• Actively listen to the clients' responses and take detailed notes.

This is perhaps the most important part of the initial consultation. When a client is speaking, don't just wait for your turn to speak, you must truly listen. I've had clients tell me years later that they chose me because I was the only planner who really heard them.

• Pay attention to their tone and body language to gauge their excitement and concerns.

Sometimes, what clients don't say is as important as what they do say. If a father tenses up when discussing certain aspects of the budget, or if an aunt seems concerned about accommodation for out-of-town guests, these are cues you need to pick up on. Being attuned to these subtle signals will help you navigate potential challenges down the line.

Remember, the initial consultation is about establishing a relationship based on trust, understanding, and shared excitement. When you show them you've understood their vision, and strike the chords that nobody else did, they are bound to want you onboard for all the weddings in their family.

| 6 |

Key Questions to Ask

The most important thing during an initial meeting is to study the client beforehand.

You can prepare a standard set of questions in advance. Tools like ChatGPT or online resources can help you create a list of questions to ask clients. The key is to read the client carefully. Most planners make the mistake of misunderstanding the client's needs. If the client wants apples, don't show them oranges.

General Information:

• **What is the date and location of your wedding?**

This seems straightforward, but it gives me crucial information. Is the date fixed because of *muhurat* considerations? Is the venue already booked, or are they looking for suggestions? If they're considering an auspicious date during wedding season, I immediately make mental notes about vendor availability and potential pricing challenges.

• **How many guests are you expecting?**

In our Indian context, this question often leads to interesting answers. I've had clients say "Just a small function, about 500 people" or "A big fat wedding, at least 1,500 guests." Understanding their definition of "small" or "big" helps me gauge their expectations. I always follow up with questions about the guest breakdown: how many from the bride's side, how many from the groom's side, and how many out-of-town guests will need accommodation.

We recently did a wedding in Mysore where the client invited 2,000 people, but 4,500 showed up. The entire road was jammed, and traffic police had to manage the area. We had to stop people from driving in and make them walk the last kilometer to the venue.

When we asked the client how did 4,500 people turn up? It turned out that the client had visited 2000 homes to share the invitation. That means 2000 families.

In a situation like that, you could either lose your mind or look at the chaos as an opportunity.

In another case, a Saudi wedding expected 4,500 guests, but 8,500 came. I called my caterer, Jawad, at 9 PM, and he said, "Brother, 4,500 plates that were guaranteed for the event are over."

It was nine o'clock.

Muslim wedding starts at nine o'clock.

I was taken aback. I asked, "Are you serious? How much food is left that we can still serve?"

The answer was 400 more plates. We had 4,500 more guests coming.

We kept cooking, but eventually, we could only serve biryani because starters and other dishes couldn't be prepared quickly. I stayed in the kitchen the entire time, eating my lunch and dinner there.

Chaos creates opportunities. Even in such situations, we managed to keep things running.

Budget:

- **How much are you willing to spend on the wedding?**

As I've said before, I always discuss budget upfront. In many cases, especially in traditional Indian families, this conversation might happen with the bride's or groom's father rather than the couple themselves. I approach this with sensitivity, understanding that discussing money can be uncomfortable for some.

- **Are there any areas where you are willing to splurge or prefer to save?**

This question reveals so much about their priorities. Some families will spend lavishly on food but are happy with simpler décor. Others might want an elaborate *Mandap* but are flexible about *mehendi* artists. I had one bride who was adamant about having a particular playback singer perform at her *sangeet,* regardless of cost but was happy to compromise on other elements.

Vision and Style:

• How would you describe the overall vision or theme for your wedding?

I love asking this question because it gets people excited. Some clients come with Pinterest boards or Instagram saves, while others simply describe a feeling they want to create. I remember a couple who said, "We want it to feel like a royal Rajasthani wedding but with modern touches." That gave me a direction to work with.

• Do you have specific colors, styles, or decor elements in mind?

Details matter. Is the bride dreaming of a particular flower for her gajra? Does the groom's mother have a preference for the *Mandap* design? Are there family traditions about certain decor elements that must be incorporated? I take careful notes because these small details often become the most meaningful aspects of the wedding.

Vendors:

• Have you already booked any vendors (venue, caterer, photographer, etc.)?

This helps me understand what pieces of the puzzle are already in place. If they've booked a photographer known for a particular style, it gives me insights into their aesthetic preferences.

• Are there any vendors you are particularly interested in?

Sometimes clients have their hearts set on working with specific vendors. It could be a *mehendi* artist who created beautiful designs for a cousin's wedding, or a caterer known for exceptional Bengali cuisine. Understanding these preferences helps me plan accordingly or suggest alternatives if their desired vendors aren't available.

Priorities and Must-Haves:

• **What are the most important aspects of your wedding to you?**

This question reveals the heart of their vision. Is it about creating Instagram-worthy moments? Is it about honoring family traditions? Is it about ensuring guests have an unforgettable culinary experience? One bride told me, "I want my grandmother, who can't travel far, to be comfortable and enjoy every moment." That single priority shaped many of our subsequent decisions.

• **Are there any elements or traditions that are essential?**

This question is crucial. Some families have specific rituals that have been followed for generations. Others might want to incorporate elements from both the bride's and groom's cultural backgrounds. Understanding these non-negotiables helps me create a plan that honors tradition while still reflecting the couple's unique story.

Timeline:

• **What is your preferred timeline for the planning process?**

Some clients come to us a year in advance, while others might be planning a wedding in just two months. Understanding their timeline helps me set realistic expectations and prioritize tasks accordingly. If we're working with a shorter timeline, I'm upfront about what's feasible and what might be challenging.

• **Are there any key dates or deadlines we need to be aware of?**

Beyond the wedding date itself, there might be other significant dates to consider. Perhaps the engagement ceremony is already scheduled, or family members from abroad will only be available during certain periods. These details help me create a comprehensive timeline that accommodates all key events.

Concerns and Challenges:

• Do you have any specific concerns or challenges regarding the wedding planning?

This question often reveals unspoken anxieties. Maybe there are family dynamics at play. Perhaps the bride's parents are divorced and seating arrangements need careful consideration. Or there might be concerns about elderly relatives who need special accommodations. By addressing these concerns early, we can develop strategies to manage them effectively.

• How involved do you want to be in the planning process?

Some clients want to be part of every decision, while others prefer to delegate everything after establishing the broad vision. I've worked with brides who wanted daily updates and others who said, "Just make it beautiful, I trust you." Understanding their desired level of involvement helps me communicate effectively throughout the planning process.

Additional Details:

• Are there any unique elements or personal touches you'd like to include?

These personal touches often become the most memorable aspects of a wedding. I've incorporated everything from a surprise performance by the groom for his bride to a replica of the restaurant where a couple had their first date. These elements transform a beautiful wedding into an unforgettable personal story.

• Do you have a backup plan for weather-related issues if your wedding is outdoors?

In India, we contend with everything from monsoon rains to extreme heat, depending on the region and season. If they're planning an outdoor function, I always discuss contingency plans. Would they be open to a tent as a backup? How would they feel about shifting certain elements indoors if necessary? Having these conversations in advance prevents last-minute stress if the weather doesn't cooperate.

Remember, these questions are just starting points. The real skill lies in actively listening to their answers and asking thoughtful follow-up questions. When you approach the initial consultation as a genuine conversation rather than a checklist, you'll gain deeper insights that will help you create a truly personalized wedding experience.

| 7 |

Understanding Client's Needs & Expectations

Imagine walking into a meeting with a client who has dreamed about their wedding day since they were a child. They have Pinterest boards, magazine cutouts, and a head full of ideas that they've been collecting for years. But here's the thing, they don't always know how to articulate what they want, or even if what they want is possible. This is where your role as a wedding planner becomes crucial.

Clarify and Confirm

I cannot stress this enough: ALWAYS repeat back what you've heard. This simple technique has saved me from countless misunderstandings and potential disasters.

During my early days, I met with a bride who kept saying she wanted a "simple, elegant wedding." I nodded along, thinking I understood perfectly. Later, when I presented my initial ideas, she looked disappointed. "This isn't what I meant by simple and elegant," she said. That's when I realized that "simple and elegant" meant different things to different people.

Now, I always say something like, "So if I understand correctly, when you say 'simple and elegant,' you're thinking of minimalist decor with white flowers, soft lighting, and no bold colors. Is that right?" This gives the client a chance to correct me or add more details.

Similarly, when a client mentions a specific color scheme, don't just note it down, show them shade cards or samples. "When you say burgundy, do you mean this shade or this one?" These small clarifications make a massive difference in the final outcome.

And don't be afraid to ask follow-up questions. If a client mentions they want a "traditional ceremony," ask what traditions are important to them. Every family has its own interpretation of tradition, and your job is to understand their specific version.

Set Expectations

This is probably the trickiest part of client management. The clients often come with ideas that are beyond their budget or technically impossible. Your job is not to crush their dreams but to help them understand what's realistic.

I remember a client who wanted an outdoor wedding in Bangalore during the monsoon season. Instead of simply saying, "That's a bad idea," I explained the risks and offered alternatives. "The rainy season can be unpredictable. If you're set on an outdoor ceremony, we can arrange a beautiful transparent tent as a backup. That way, you get the outdoor feel while staying protected."

When discussing budgets, be transparent about costs. If a client wants a wedding with 500 guests but has a budget for 200, help them understand where they need to compromise. "With your current budget, we can have 500 guests with simpler food options, or we can have 200 guests with the premium menu you wanted. Which would you prefer?"

Remember, setting realistic expectations doesn't mean saying "no". It means finding creative solutions that align with the client's vision and budget.

Offer Suggestions

This is where your creativity and experience truly shine. Based on what the client has shared, offer suggestions that enhance their vision.

For instance, if a bride mentions she loves flowers but is concerned about the cost, suggest mixing real flowers with high-quality artificial ones in less noticeable areas. Or if a groom wants a grand entrance but the venue doesn't support it, propose alternative ideas that achieve the same wow factor.

I once had a client who was adamant about having a beach wedding, but the logistics were proving to be a nightmare. Instead of dismissing their wish, I suggested creating a beach-like setting with sand, palm trees, and ocean sounds at a more accessible location. They loved the idea, and the guests were amazed by the transformation.

Your suggestions should always come from a place of enhancing the client's vision, not replacing it. The goal is to help them realize their dream in the most practical and effective way possible.

Establish Communication

Clear communication is the backbone of successful event planning. In your first meeting, establish how and when you'll communicate.

Some clients prefer weekly email updates, while others want phone calls or face-to-face meetings. Ask them directly, "How would you prefer we stay in touch? Would you like regular updates, or should I contact you only when decisions need to be made?"

I typically suggest a weekly update email with a quick call if needed. This keeps the client informed without overwhelming them with daily details. For major decisions, I always prefer in-person meetings where we can discuss options and make choices together.

Also, make it clear who the point of contact will be. As I mentioned earlier, having one person as the decision-maker prevents confusion and conflicting instructions. "To keep things streamlined, who should I contact with updates and questions? And who will have the final say in decisions?"

At least a month before the wedding, increase the frequency of updates. This ensures everyone is on the same page as the big day approaches.

Next Steps

Never end a meeting without a clear plan for what happens next. Summarize what was discussed and outline the immediate action items.

After finalizing the presentation (PPT) with the client, you start discussing the details. The PPT usually includes multiple options for each element — backdrops, props, photo booths, masking, ceiling designs, etc. You go through each element one by one, discussing what they like and what they don't. For some clients, we create 3D renders to help them visualize the setup. Others trust us completely and say, "We can't visualize it. You know your job better. Just go ahead and do it."

The biggest challenge here is the time it takes for detailing. Sometimes, it can take 8–12 hours or even span multiple days. I've had situations where I've slept, woken up, and continued working the next day to finish the detailing. For high-budget weddings, this process can take 3–4 days because there are so many elements involved. And, of course, things keep changing. Different family members have different opinions, and you have to navigate through all of that.

How do you handle unrealistic requests from clients?

There are times when a client will ask you for absurd arrangements. If a client asks for something unrealistic, I usually give them an unrealistic quote. For example, if they want a gold-plated ceiling, I'll say, "This will cost you Rupees 50 lakhs. Do you want it?" Usually, they'll say, "No, no, drop that."

This may sound humorous and unrealistic, but this is exactly how it needs to be handled. Otherwise, you may end up losing your mind and money fulfilling unreasonable demands.

However, not all demands are unreasonable. If the client wants to change something and I know the material can be reused in the future, I'll say, "It's okay. I've already invested in it, so I'll keep it and won't charge you." But if the material is something I can't reuse, I'll be firm and say, "We've already bought it, so we'll have to include the cost in the decor." No client will ever say, "Don't add it to the decor" if you've already bought it. They'll always agree to include it in the wedding.

MODULE 3

BUDGETING

"Weddings are not about spending the least amount of money or the most amount of money; they are about spending good money on the elements that are most important to you and your partner."

- ***Kristi Richardson***

| 8 |

The Importance of a Wedding Budget

Most planners won't admit this, but in reality, we've seen more weddings derailed by poor budgeting than by any other factor.

You can have the most beautiful concept, the most talented vendors, and the most excited couple, but if the money runs out halfway through, everything falls apart. I've witnessed families taking loans, selling assets, and even postponing weddings because they didn't plan their finances properly. Trust me, you don't want to be in that position.

When I first meet clients, they've attended some gorgeous wedding setups, seen lavish weddings on Instagram, and they think, "That's what I want!"

But that floating stage with a thousand lotus flowers they saw? It may cost more than their entire budget.

That's why I always start by asking, "How much are you comfortable spending on this wedding?" Notice I didn't say, "What's your budget?" Because when you ask that, people immediately go on the defensive, thinking you're trying to extract as much money as possible from them.

Instead, I frame it as a comfort level. This approach makes clients more forthcoming about their financial situation. Once I know their range, I can guide them accordingly. If they say Rupees 20 lakhs but want a wedding that costs Rupees 40 lakhs, I immediately flag this discrepancy rather than pretending it's possible.

You can't get a BMW in the budget of a Maruti. If you still need a BMW in the budget of a Maruti, you can get yourself a fourth-hand BMW.

While working with a client, this is how we approach the budgeting. We ask the client for the budget, curate things according to it and give it to them. If we feel that their vision and their budget don't match, I openly & humbly tell them "Sir, your vision doesn't match your budget. For the vision you have, this is the budget that you need."

The only two scenarios that can follow this discussion is either you can increase the budget or you can change the vision.

They either increase the budget or adjust their vision.

Financial Planning

Financial planning involves breaking down every expense like decor, sound, lighting, etc. You get quotes from vendors, negotiate, and then add a markup for your profit. On top of the rates you've received from the vendors & your profit margin (which could be 20% - 100%), you add a negotiation buffer of 20%.

I always keep a 20% negotiation buffer, because when a client negotiates you can offer them a 10% discount. And only if a client negotiates frugally, you offer them additional 10% discount.

Prioritization

Every couple has different priorities. Some want an elaborate *Mandap*, others care more about food, and some are focused on photography. A budget helps identify these priorities and allocate funds accordingly.

I always ask my clients to rank these aspects in order of importance:

- Venue
- Decor
- Food & Beverages
- Photography & Videography
- Entertainment
- Attire
- Accommodations
- Transportation
- Gifts & Favors

Once we have this ranking, we can allocate a higher percentage of the budget to the top three items and find ways to save on the rest.

For example, I had a couple who were foodies. The groom was a chef, and both families had a deep appreciation for cuisine. They decided to allocate 40% of their budget to food and beverages, which meant scaling back on some decor elements.

Their wedding might not have had the most elaborate decorations, but the seven-course meal prepared by celebrity chefs became the talk of the town. Every guest remembered the experience, which was exactly what the couple wanted.

Similarly, another client was a photographer himself. For him, documenting the wedding was paramount. We allocated a significant portion of the budget to hire the best photography and videography team, even bringing them in from another city. The photos and videos were museum-quality, capturing moments that the family will cherish forever.

A budget doesn't just tell you how much you can spend. It tells you where you should spend it.

Decision-Making

Weddings involve hundreds of decisions, from the major (venue, date, guest list) to the minor (napkin color, welcome drink options, playlist). Without a budget framework, these decisions become overwhelming.

When a client is torn between two venues, I can show them how each choice impacts the overall budget. If Venue A costs Rupees 5 lakhs more than Venue B, I help them understand what else they might have to sacrifice if they choose A. Perhaps it means simpler centerpieces or dropping the idea of welcome gifts. This clarity helps them make informed decisions rather than emotional ones.

I've found that having a budget spreadsheet that we update regularly keeps everyone grounded. After each major decision, we revisit the spreadsheet to see how it affected our available funds.

Vendor Negotiations

This is where many planners go wrong. They approach vendors without a clear budget in mind, hear a price, and then try to haggle it down. This rarely works well.

Instead, I approach vendors with clarity: "We have Rupees X for decor. What can you provide within this budget that aligns with our theme?" This transparency often leads to more creative solutions and better collaboration.

Vendors appreciate clients who are upfront about their budget constraints.

That said, I also caution against always choosing the cheapest option. As I mentioned earlier, quality comes at a price. If a vendor's quote seems significantly lower than others, there's usually a reason. They might be using subpar materials, inexperienced staff, or cutting corners in ways that will show on the day.

When negotiating, focus on value rather than just price.

I once worked with a decor vendor who initially quoted Rupees 7 lakhs for a setup. When I explained our budget constraints, instead of simply reducing the quality, they suggested using the same premium materials but in a more focused way. The vision was to create one statement piece that would be the highlight, rather than trying to decorate the entire venue elaborately. The result was actually more impactful than the original plan, and within budget.

| 9 |

Tips for Creating & Managing a Wedding

Indian weddings are particularly challenging to budget because of our expansive celebrations that often span multiple days with various ceremonies.

Determine Total Budget

Wedding budgets often involve multiple family members contributing. Start by having a frank conversation with all contributing parties. I've seen too many misunderstandings where the groom's parents assumed the bride's family would cover certain expenses based on tradition, or vice versa. These assumptions can lead to last-minute financial stress.

Create a clear list of who's contributing what. If the bride's maternal uncle is covering the *sangeet* venue, get that commitment in writing with a specific amount. If the groom's parents are handling all the accommodation costs for their guests, define exactly what "accommodation" includes. Does it cover transportation from the airport? Welcome baskets? Room service?

For couples managing their own weddings, be realistic about your savings and avoid dipping into your future funds. I've had clients who wanted to use their home down payment savings for their wedding.

I always advise against this. Your wedding is a celebration of your future together, it shouldn't compromise that future.

Break Down the Budget

- **Venue and Catering (40-45%):** This typically covers the main wedding venue, food, and beverages for all functions.
- **Decor (15-20%):** Including *Mandap,* stage setup, lighting, and floral arrangements.
- **Attire and Jewelry (15%):** For bride, groom, and sometimes immediate family members.
- **Photography and Videography (8-10%):** Including pre-wedding shoots, which are now standard.
- **Entertainment (5-8%):** DJs, live bands, *sangeet* choreographers, and traditional musicians.
- **Invitations and Stationery (3-5%):** Wedding cards, which are still important despite digital alternatives.
- **Miscellaneous (5%):** Including *Mehendi* artists, makeup artists, and transportation.
- **Contingency (5-10%):** Always set aside this buffer.

I had clients from Rajasthan who were surprised that decor took up so much of their budget. In their community, weddings traditionally focused more on food and hospitality than elaborate decorations. Conversely, I've worked with families from Gujarat who prioritized entertainment and were willing to allocate nearly 15% of their budget to it.

The key is to align the budget breakdown with your priorities and cultural expectations. There's no one-size-fits-all approach.

Track Expenses

Indian weddings have a notorious way of expanding beyond initial plans. That modest 200-person guest list somehow becomes 350. The two-day celebration extends to four days of events. Without diligent tracking, costs spiral quickly.

Create a detailed spreadsheet with multiple sheets:

- One for each major function (*Mehendi, Sangeet,* Wedding, Reception)
- One for attire expenses
- One for vendor deposits and payment schedules
- One summary sheet that pulls from all others
- Update this spreadsheet religiously. After every vendor meeting, every purchase, every decision, go back to your spreadsheet.

I recommend using cloud-based tools like Google Sheets so multiple family members can access and update the budget. This creates accountability and transparency.

One of my clients, a software engineer from Bangalore, created an impressive tracking system with automated alerts when they approached category limits. While that level of sophistication isn't necessary, the principle is sound: know where your money is going.

Include a Contingency Fund

In weddings, unexpected expenses are not just possible, they're guaranteed. Perhaps the groom's family decides last minute that they want to add a welcome ceremony the day before the main events. Or maybe an important family elder arrives with their entire family, adding 15 people to your guest count overnight.

I always set aside 10% of the total budget as a contingency. In the rare cases where we don't use it, the couple has extra money for their honeymoon or new home.

A family I worked with from Chennai had set aside Rupees 3 lakhs as contingency. When unexpected rains damaged some of their outdoor decor the night before the wedding, we were able to quickly arrange alternatives without causing financial stress or compromising on quality.

Review and Adjust

Schedule formal budget reviews with all decision-makers at these milestones:

- After booking major vendors (venue, catering)
- Halfway through the planning process
- One month before the wedding
- Immediately after the wedding (to settle final payments)

During these reviews, be honest about where you stand. If you've overspent in one category, decide immediately where you'll cut back to compensate.

I had a couple who splurged on a designer *lehenga* that was Rupees 2 lakhs over their attire budget. During our review, they decided to scale back their reception decor from grand floral arrangements to more subtle and elegant styling. The end result still looked beautiful, and their budget remained balanced as well.

Unexpected Shock in the Budget

Yes, it happens. For example, a vendor might back out last minute or realize that they underestimated the cost. Once, a vendor quoted Rupees 30,000 for a backdrop but later said it would cost Rupees 50,000. In such cases, I either absorb the extra cost from my profit or find ways to adjust it elsewhere in the budget. Being honest to the client also matters. If the client is understanding, I explain the situation and give them the option to pay the difference. However, if they are firm, I must manage it myself.

Another challenge is the fluctuating flower prices. Flowers are like the stock market; their prices change daily. Once, I quoted Rupees 350 per bunch of roses (20 roses per bunch), but due to a shortage, the price shot up to Rupees 750. The entire wedding was based on real flowers. The client refused to pay extra, and I ended up losing Rupees 9 lakhs on that wedding.

It was tough, but I learned to develop contingency plans.

Another scenario occurred March 16, 2020. A naming ceremony for the Reddy's. It was the MLA whose son's naming ceremony was getting planned. Considering in the contingency cost, I quoted a price of a surplus of Rupees 50 per bunch of flowers. When we talk about Reddy's, they are known to go big on real flower decors.

I had quoted Rupees 250 per bunch of flowers, expecting the price to drop to Rupees 150–200. But COVID happened, many weddings were cancelled. The rates we got for the flowers were...can you take a guess? Rupees 25 per bunch. That was 1/10th the expected price. And how many flowers were we using? 1 Lakh.

I felt it was God's plan because the money we made helped us feed the workers during COVID.

The profits helped us survive the lockdown. I couldn't send my workers back home because the trains were cancelled. However, I sent rations to their families so that they could survive these tough times.

Before COVID, I didn't do B2B business. I was a wedding planner with my own decor team. However, everything changed during the lockdown.

At that time, no other wedding planners had the capability to execute weddings. There were no workers, decorators, or laborers. They had returned to their villages, except for my team, which I could keep owing to God's blessings.

One wedding was booked for April 27, 2020. The couple had to get married on that date for astrological reasons, or they'd have to wait three years. They obtained special permission and decided to hold the wedding at home. We used artificial flowers with minimal decor, and the wedding went smoothly.

I then began posting about "lockdown weddings" on social media. A friend shared my work in a major media publication. Not only was this a proud moment, but it was an opportunity that I grabbed. I started sharing that article with every group and associations I was a part of.

It spread like wildfire. Families started calling me for small, intimate weddings at home, on terraces, in parking lots—anywhere you can think of. I even performed a wedding on a road!

My phone started buzzing with calls from other wedding planners and event managers who wanted us to take up the weddings.

This is how my B2B business started. During COVID, I became one of the busiest wedding planners in the country, handling three to four weddings a week. Currently, 98% of my business is B2B, and only 2% is direct client work.

| 10 |

Common Expenses in Indian Weddings

Venue

In metropolitan cities such as Mumbai, Delhi, and Bangalore, venue costs can consume up to 30% of the total budget. The pricing varies dramatically based on the season.

Tips:

- Consider hosting your wedding during the summer months (April-June), when demand is lower due to the heat.
- Explore venues in satellite cities. A wedding in Noida rather than Delhi center could save you 30-40% on venue costs.
- For destination weddings, consider Rajasthan during the monsoon (July-September) or Goa during the shoulder season (October or February).
- Weekday weddings are becoming more acceptable and can save you 25-30% on venue costs.

Catering

Food is non-negotiable at Indian weddings. Guests might forgive average decor, but they will remember poor food forever.

Tips:

- Instead of a fully open bar, offer selected drinks such as beer, wine, and two signature cocktails.
- For multiple functions, the cuisine style should be varied rather than the quality. Perhaps a Rajasthani thali for one function and an international buffet for another would be ideal.
- Consider serving premium food but limiting its variety. Five excellent dishes impress more than twenty mediocre ones.
- Breakfast and lunch events are significantly cheaper than dinner events.

Attire

Indian wedding attire, especially bridal wear, can be surprisingly expensive, with designer *lehengas* easily costing Rupees 5 lakhs or more.

Tips:

- Consider renting bridal jewelry instead of buying new pieces.
- Look at emerging designers who offer quality craftsmanship at lower prices than established names.
- For the groom, investing in a high-quality sherwani that can be reworn for other functions is better option than buying multiple outfits.
- Family members can coordinate colors rather than buying identical outfits, allowing them to use pieces they might already own.

Photography and Videography

With social media's influence, this category has grown substantially in terms of importance and cost.

Tips:

- Book photographers for specific hours rather than full days.
- Skip the elaborate pre-wedding shoot in exotic locations and opt for a simpler session at a meaningful local spot.
- Prioritize the main photographer's time for key ceremonies and portrait sessions.
- Consider hiring a separate team for candid photography rather than paying premium rates for the main team to cover everything.

Entertainment

From DJs to live bands to celebrity performers, entertainment costs can vary dramatically.

Tips:

- Showcase family talent during the *sangeet* instead of hiring professional performers.
- For *sangeet* choreography, hire a choreographer for one session to teach family members the routine rather than booking multiple sessions.
- Use a curated playlist for pre and post-ceremony gatherings, saving the DJ for the main reception.
- Traditional folk musicians often charge less than contemporary bands but add authentic cultural elements to your celebration.

Decorations

Decor expectations have skyrocketed with social media, but there are ways to create an impact without breaking the bank.

Tips:

- Focus on creating one or two "wow" moments rather than decorating every inch of the venue.
- Use more lighting and fabric draping, which can be reused across functions, rather than fresh flowers that need to be replaced daily.
- For *Mandaps*, consider a semi-permanent structure that can be enhanced differently for each ceremony, rather than building separate *Mandaps*.
- In-season local flowers are significantly cheaper than imported varieties.

Stationery

Despite the digital revolution, physical invitations remain important in Indian culture.

Tips:

- Send elaborate physical invitations only to close family members and elders who value tradition.
- Use digital invitations for younger guests and for distant relatives.
- Instead of multiple inserts, create a wedding website with all the details about the various functions.
- Consider box invitations only for VIP guests and simplified versions for others.

Transportation

With multiple venues and hotels, transportation logistics can become complicated and expensive for both the family and the organizers.

Tips:

- Choose venues close to accommodation to minimize transportation requirements.
- For destination weddings,group transportation should be organized rather than individual pickups.
- If providing transportation for all guests isn't feasible, prioritize elderly family members, out-of-town guests, and the wedding party.
- Create a detailed transportation schedule and share it in advance to avoid last-minute confusion and additional vehicles.

Favors and Gifts

Return gifts and favors are a significant aspect of Indian weddings.

Tips:

- Opt for the meaningful over the expensive. A custom spice blend made from a family recipe can be more memorable than generic luxury items.
- For destination weddings, incorporate local specialties as gifts to guests.
- Consider giving different gifts for different categories of guests rather than the same expensive items for everyone.
- Handwritten notes with simple gifts add a personal touch without incurring significant costs.

| 11 |

Cost Saving Tips for Indian Weddings

Prioritize and Trim

Be brutally honest about what matters the most. Is having a celebrity performer worth cutting corners on food quality? Is an elaborately embroidered *lehenga* worth settling for a less prestigious venue?

I had clients who were passionate about music and had their hearts set on a famous Sufi singer for their *sangeet* ceremony. To accommodate this within their budget, they simplified their *mehendi* function to a home event rather than a separate venue-function. The result was a memorable *sangeet* that guests still talk about and an intimate, meaningful *mehendi* ceremony with close family.

DIY Projects

Some clients want to do DIY projects, especially housewives who want to add a personal touch to the wedding. Although it is time-consuming, we support them if they're passionate about it.

Small elements such as favor packaging, welcome baskets, and simple decor items, can be DIY projects. I had a bride whose family created beautiful potli bags filled with traditional sweets as wedding favors. Not only did it save money, but it became a bonding activity for the women in the family.

Limit Guest List

This is perhaps the most challenging aspect of Indian weddings, where guest lists of 500+ are common. However, it's also the most effective way to control costs, as nearly every expense scales with the guest count.

Consider hosting multiple smaller celebrations instead of a single large event. Perhaps an intimate ceremony with just 50-100 close family members, followed by a larger reception or multiple regional receptions if families are from different cities.

I worked with a couple who organized a small destination wedding in Udaipur with just 80 guests, followed by reception parties in Delhi and Bangalore, where their extended families lived. Despite hosting multiple events, they saved significantly on accommodation and transportation costs.

Negotiate with Vendors

In India, negotiations are expected. However, the focus should be on finding win-win solutions rather than simply demanding discounts.

For example, rather than asking a photographer to lower their rate, ask if they can include an additional hour of coverage or an extra photo album for the same price. With decorators, we can evaluate whether elements from one function can be repurposed for another at a reduced cost.

I once negotiated with a venue to waive their outside vendor fee in exchange for booking all three days of wedding functions. Both parties felt that they gained value from the arrangement.

Combine Services

Look for vendors who offer multiple services. Many decor companies now handle lighting as well. Some caterers can provide bar services along with food.

This not only potentially reduces costs but also simplifies coordination, as you're dealing with fewer vendors overall.

Borrow or Rent

When it comes to decor, renting is often better than buying. If the rental cost is 10–20% of the buying price, it makes sense to rent. For example, if a sofa rental costs Rupees 10,000 but making it costs Rupees 20,000, I'll get it made. If I use it twice, it pays for itself, and every use after that is a profit.

However, for fragile items like glassware, it's better to rent because they often break during transport.

Borrowing and renting can also apply to jewelry. Bridal jewelry, especially pieces worn only for the ceremony, can often be borrowed from family members, adding sentimental value while saving substantial amounts of money.

Similarly, renting *baraat* elements such as *ghodi* (horse) or vintage cars, which are used for very short durations, can be considered.

Remember, a wedding is ultimately about celebrating relationships and bringing families together. A thoughtfully planned event within your client's means will create far more joy than an extravagant celebration that leaves them financially stressed.

In my years of planning weddings across India and internationally, I've seen that the most memorable celebrations are rarely the most expensive ones. They're the ones where the couple's personality shines through, where guests feel genuinely welcomed and included, and where the focus remains on the meaning of the occasion rather than just its appearance.

Plan wisely, spend intentionally, and the wedding will be remembered for all the right reasons.

MODULE 4

VENUE SELECTION

"Weddings are made of love, but wedding planners make them happen."-**Unknown**

| 12 |

Choosing a Venue That Actually Works

You see a five-star venue. Polished floors, grand chandeliers, and fancy floral installations from their last wedding still hanging at the entrance. You think, "This is it."

That's where most newbies go wrong.

What looks good in pictures might create chaos in real life if you're not careful.

I've even seen planners push venues just because they're getting a fat commission, even if it makes zero sense for the client's needs. That's not only poor planning. That's selfish planning.

Not to mention, most clients have no clue how to choose the right venue. They'll go ahead with what you recommend, but this will add to the realtime chaos.

That said, you should also clearly communicate your requirements to the client before finalising the venue. For example, tell them upfront:

- I'll need a dumping area.
- I'll need a smaller utility room.
- I'll need 4–5 rooms for my staff.

If it's a two-day or three-day wedding, all these details need to be clearly communicated before any venue is locked in.

Don't wait till the venue is finalised to bring these up. Lay everything on the table early so there are no surprises later.

| 13 |

Factors to Consider When Choosing a Venue

Location

- Proximity to guests and accommodations.
- Accessibility for guests traveling from out of town.

Capacity

- Ensure the venue can comfortably accommodate the guest list.
- Consider space for the ceremony, reception, and other activities.
- A venue might claim it can host 500 guests, but after allocating space for the stage, buffet, bar, and dance floor, you're left with room for 250. Always do a layout walkthrough.

Budget

- Align venue cost with the overall wedding budget. Don't recommend a Rupees 25L venue to a Rupees 15L client just because it looks pretty. You'll spend the rest of the planning phase justifying every rupee.
- Include all associated fees (rental, setup, cleanup).
- Always ask for a detailed cost breakdown: rental, service charge, taxes, cleaning fee, overtime charges, corkage fees (yes, even that), and any "security deposits." Ask what happens if you

exceed time limits. Some venues will charge penalties quietly hidden in the contract.

Style and Ambiance

- Match the venue's style with the wedding theme and couple's vision.
- Consider the venue's architecture, decor, and overall vibe.
- Some venues have poor lighting or overpowering chandeliers. Visit in the evening and check the vibe. What looks dreamy at noon might be dull after sunset.

Amenities and Services

- Check for included amenities (tables, chairs, linens, sound system).
- Power and backup (How many plug points? Do they have generators? Who pays for fuel? Ask these before you sign anything.)
- Look for on-site services (catering, event coordination).

Most venues will have someone designated to help with event execution, either an event manager or the banquet team. Sit with them. Ask what's allowed and what's not. Trust me, there are always *restrictions.*

They're the ones who'll tell you:

- Can you drill into the wall for a hanging decor piece?
- Can you use the pool deck for a *haldi*?
- What time do they shut down music?
- Which areas are off-limits?

Some hotels will tell you *yes* to everything when you're making the booking and *no* to everything two days before the wedding. Ask me how I know.

Availability:

- Confirm the venue's availability on the desired wedding date. Some venues get booked a year in advance.
- Consider flexibility for preferred dates or seasons. If the client is open to multiple dates or mid-week weddings that can sometimes come at lower costs.

Logistics:

- Ensure adequate parking or transportation options for guests. If your venue only offers 40–50 car slots for a 500-guest wedding, your guests will end up doing circles on the street. Always confirm: how many vehicles? Is valet included? Is there overflow parking?
- Check for accommodations nearby if needed.

Weather and Backup Plan:

- For outdoor venues, ensure there is a backup plan for inclement weather.
- Check for indoor spaces or tenting options. Check if they allow external tent vendors or insist on in-house. What's the cost? How quickly can it be set up in an emergency?

Restrictions:

- Be aware of any venue restrictions (noise, decor, timing). Can you bring your own caterer, decorator, DJ, or bar team? Or are you locked into their in-house vendors? Some venues charge a fee for using external teams.
- Understand policies regarding outside vendors and alcohol.

Reviews and Reputation:

- Research online reviews and testimonials.
- Seek recommendations from friends, family, or wedding planners.

A good venue makes your job 10X easier.

What Other Planners Won't Tell You: Talk to People Who've Been There

Before finalising a venue, talk to other planners who've worked there. Not the sales team. Not the website. The **people who've run actual weddings** there.

They'll give you the real picture of what works, what doesn't, which side has more mosquito trouble, how cooperative (or not) the staff is, and whether or not the manager disappears during the main event.

That kind of inside information is gold.

Before locking the venue, bring in your **decor team**, **sound & lights**, and **logistics head** for a quick walkthrough. They'll notice things you won't, like lack of backstage space, inaccessible load-in zones, or power supply issues.

This one step can save you from massive chaos later.

Venue Logistics: Parking, Buggies & The Great Innova

Guest experience starts the moment they reach the venue—not when the ceremony begins.

- Is there ample parking?
- Are valet services included?
- Does the venue provide buggies or will you need to arrange them?

Let me tell you, buggies > Innovas. Always. If your venue has multiple zones, or if you're coordinating between hotel and function venues, don't default to Innovas or sedans.

Because some guests don't want to sit with people they don't know, or worse, don't *like*. I've literally seen family members refusing to board a car because of someone sitting inside. You don't want to manage that drama on the day.

Buggies are a smarter choice. They're open, neutral, easy to access, and ideal for quick shuttles within venue premises.

| 14 |

Venue Visit Checklist

Here's a simple rule: **create a checklist**. Then create a checklist for the checklist. You can create your own checklist if you'd like or you can use mine:

General Questions:

- Is the venue available on the preferred date?
- What is the total capacity of the venue?

Costs and Fees:

- What is the rental fee, and what does it include?
- Are there additional costs (cleaning, security, overtime)?

Space and Layout:

- Are there separate areas for the ceremony, cocktail hour, and reception?
- Is there a designated area for dancing and entertainment?

Services and Amenities:

- What furniture and equipment are included (tables, chairs, linens)?
- Are there in-house catering and bar services? Can we bring our own?

Logistics:

- Is there ample parking or valet service available?
- Are there nearby accommodations for out-of-town guests?

Staff and Coordination:

- Is there an on-site coordinator or event manager?
- What level of support will they provide on the wedding day?

Restrictions and Policies:

- Are there any noise restrictions or curfews?
- What are the policies on outside vendors and decor?

Backup Plans:

- What is the backup plan for bad weather if the venue has outdoor spaces?
- Are there additional costs associated with backup plans?

Accessibility:

- Is the venue accessible for guests with disabilities?
- Are there adequate restroom facilities for all guests?

Contract Details:

- What is the payment schedule and cancellation policy?
- Are there any insurance requirements?

The 50 Decibel Disaster

There was this one time where the hotel said, "Sound is allowed outside." Perfect, I thought. We planned an open-air musical evening.

But just two days before the event, they brought out the contract and said, "Yes, but only up to 50 decibels."

Now let me explain what 50 decibels sounds like, it's me and you talking quietly. That's it. So, no music. And no music means no vibe.

Can you imagine a *baraat* with 50 decibel music? Might as well give guests wireless headphones and play the *dhol* in their imagination.

I asked the venue managers, "Then what's the point of saying sound is allowed?"

Here's what they said, "It's in the contract. You signed it."

Technically, it wasn't me. Because the client had booked the venue directly.

I asked the hotel, "What do I need to do if I want to go above 50 decibels?" They said: "Get a **police NOC** (No Objection Certificate)."

The outdoor area was managed by the **Apartment Association** of the larger property. And guess what? I had previously worked as a vendor for them. So I called the person in charge and explained the situation.

He said and quoted: "Zubair bhai, if you're handling the event, I trust you. Just get the NOC, and you're good."

And that's how we pulled it off. But **not everyone will be that lucky**.

That's why I always read venue contracts like my life depends on it. Hidden clauses, fine print, and vague restrictions, they're all in there.

Clients usually assume things are fine if they've had a good meeting. But they don't understand contracts. You, as the planner, have to protect them, even if they don't know they need protecting.

Watch Out for These Red Flags in Contracts

Here's a list of things you **must** double-check before you sign any venue deal:

- **Sound Restrictions**: Check for outdoor sound limits and time cutoffs. Ask what happens if you go beyond.
- **Cancellation Policy**: Do you get a refund? A credit note? Or nothing at all?
- **Area Access**: Which parts of the venue are you allowed to use? Are there any "off-limits" zones?

- **Decor Limitations**: Can you hang from walls, pillars, or ceilings? Any restrictions on nails or rigging?
- **Power Supply**: Backup generators? Who's responsible? You or the venue?
- **Load-in/Load-out Timings**: Do you get venue access the night before? Or only on the event day?

The Love Story That Never Happened

Sometimes, life throws you a curveball. I remember prepping for a wedding scheduled on April 19, 20, and 21. I saw the couple, and they were head over heels in love. Holding hands, forehead kisses, smiles all around. This is a rare sight in arranged marriage. I even joked that they looked too in love. Maybe my *nazar* caught them.

I was helping out as a friend, not the official planner. But I was coordinating things. Then… the wedding got called off.

Yup. Just like that. I don't know the full story. I didn't even ask who ended up paying for the venue. But everything was booked, the advance was paid, and then it was all over. Welcome to real life.

That's why cancellation policies are **not optional**. Some venues will give you a refund if it's far in advance. Others only give you a credit note. Sounds fair in theory. Because no client wants to reuse a credit note for a wedding that didn't happen.

And some will say, "Sorry sir, it's in the contract; you signed it."

Read the contract. Then read it again.

This is not a joke.

Read. Every. Line. Of. That. Contract.

Most planners walk into venue negotiations thinking they're just locking in a date and getting a hall. But if there's one thing I've learnt, it's that **the most expensive mistakes are hidden in the fine print**. Right there in the black-and-white contract you signed without asking, *"Sir, 50 decibels means what exactly?"*

Let's talk about the mess that no one prepares you for. **Venue contracts, cancellation policies, and the sneaky tactics hotels sometimes pull when you least expect it.**

| 15 |

Negotiation Is a Game of Respect, Not Desperation

Every planner thinks they know how to negotiate. Until they walk into a hotel and get steamrolled by a slick-talking sales executive who quotes Rupees 10 lakhs for something worth Rupees 4.5 lakhs.

The Truth About Sales Teams: They Quote High. Always.

Salespeople are trained to sell you everything they possibly can and at the highest possible rate. That's their job.

What you need to remember is this: **they always leave room to come down**. The initial quote is never the final one. It's their version of starting with an anchor and then making you feel like you "won" by getting it reduced.

Don't get emotionally attached to that first number. Just smile and start working the math.

How well you negotiate depends heavily on your **relationship with the venue's sales team**. If they trust you, they'll stretch their limits. If you've worked with them before and delivered well-managed events, they know you're not messing around.

But if they've never heard of you, or worse, if you come off as pushy or desperate, they won't budge.

A Real-Life Scene: When One Door Closes, Another Hotel Opens

Here's what happened during one particular wedding. We were trying to finalise a venue, and my staff was handling the negotiations. The point of contact was someone I knew, a friend, actually. But he was playing hard to get.

He kept saying, "Bhai, this budget won't work." "This rate is too low." "We can't go this low."

My team tried. He didn't move. They finally came to me and said, "Zubair bhai, he's not listening. You'll need to step in."

I picked up the phone, spoke to him politely. Still no change.

At that point, I didn't waste time. I went to another hotel. Sat down with their sales manager and said, "This is my client's budget. This is her requirement. This is what I need. If you can meet this, I'll close it *today.*"

She took five minutes. Went back. Spoke to her higher-ups. Returned and said: "Sir, can we increase slightly on one or two line items?"

I said no. Clear and firm. There was a moment of silence. Then she said, "Okay. Done. Let's close it."

What happened next is classic.

Four days later, my friend from the first hotel messaged me, "Bhai, you should have told me you were finalising elsewhere."

I replied, "I *did* come to you. You didn't budge. What else was I supposed to do?"

He responded, "But I had blocked the date for you."

And I said, "I never asked you to block anything. I was still negotiating. You assumed I'd confirm. That's not how I work."

That is the lesson from the industry. **Never assume a deal is done until it's actually done**. And never expect people to wait if you're not willing to move.

Key Takeaways for Planners Who Want to Master the Venue Contracts

Seek Inclusions:

- Ask if additional services or amenities can be included at no extra cost (extra hours, additional furniture).

Discuss Policies:

- Negotiate policies on cancellation, change of date, and refunds.
- Ensure you are comfortable with the terms before signing.

Get Everything in Writing:

- Confirm all negotiated terms in the final contract.
- Make sure any verbal agreements are included in writing.

This is the golden rule: if it's not written down, it doesn't exist.

Sometimes, hotel managers agree to something verbally just to close the deal. Later, they check with their senior team and come back with a new version of the story. So, always send a post-meeting MOM (Minutes of Meeting) to the hotel team confirming what was discussed.

Assumptions Will Kill You: So Ask the Right Questions

This had once happened with us. The venue said, "You can use the lawn."

So what do you assume? You assume you can do **decor, setup lighting, place speakers**, everything. We did too.

But later they said, "We said you can *use* the lawn. We didn't say you can do *decor* on it."

See the problem? That's why you need to follow up with:

- "Can we do decor here?"
- "Can we set up lighting and sound?"
- "Can we place trusses, floral setups, or seating arrangements?"

The more you clarify now, the smoother the event will be later.

Your foundation is your venue. Don't build it on loose sand. When things go wrong at the venue, everything falls apart. So be meticulous. Because if the foundation is weak, no amount of beautiful *Mandap* decor can save the day.

Review with a Professional:

If the wedding budget is over Rupees 2 crores and your venue deal is worth Rupees 40–50 lakhs or more, **spend Rupees 3,000–5,000 on a lawyer** to review the contract.

That small fee can save you lakhs in damages, confusion, or legal issues.

It's not compulsory. But it's *highly recommended.*

Today, you even have tools like ChatGPT. You can upload the contract and ask it to summarize the risky points. You can prompt it to highlight what works in your favor and what doesn't.

You're not here to win. You're here to make it work for your client, your team, and your business.

I've had deals fall through. I've had last-minute miracles. I've had venues that wouldn't budge give me the best rates six months later.

It's not about tricks. It's about trust. And if you handle negotiations with clarity, calm, and confidence, you'll always walk out with your head held high and your deal done right.

The Hidden Cost: Recci (Recce) Nights

When you're managing a big wedding, you'll likely have to visit the property multiple times, that's what we call *recci nights.*

These are visits to inspect the venue, plan logistics, finalise layouts, and coordinate with vendors. **Some venues include recci stays free of cost**, while others offer **heavily discounted rates**.

It all depends on:

- The scale of the wedding,

- Your relationship with the hotel,
- And frankly, your negotiation skills.

This should always be part of your venue contract discussion. Why? Because if the client refuses to pay for recci nights later, who's covering that cost? You. From your fee.

Some clients will subtly try to push that cost onto the planner, so be careful. **Don't take that responsibility silently.**

Ask for Extras, At No Extra Cost

You're not being greedy. You're being smart.

Ask the hotel if they can include **additional services like:**

- Ironing and laundry services for guests
- Extended hours without overtime charges
- Extra furniture or support staff

If they can't provide laundry or ironing, ask them for a small room in the basement or parking area where you can set up **external vendors** for this. Believe me, **ironing services are a lifesaver** during weddings, especially for guests who've just arrived from out of town.

MODULE 5

PLANNING THE DETAILS

*You can do anything, but you can't do everything-**Unknown***

| 16 |

Importance of Wedding Theme & Design

A wedding without clarity is a wedding headed for chaos. And a wedding theme gives you that clarity. When done right, a theme becomes the backbone of decision-making for the entire event. It simplifies planning, guides the decor, defines the artist lineup, and even influences things like attire, menu, and bar setup.

If your client says they want a Sufi-themed evening, you're not calling in a rock band for that night. You need a Sufi artist, the right instruments, ambient lighting, a softer colour palette, and everything needs to flow in the same direction.

That's the power of a well-defined theme. But not every client will make it this smooth for you.

You'll meet clients who've gone through 20 mood boards, seen every wedding reel on Instagram, and still, they'll sit in front of you and say, *"This isn't working."*

They don't know what they want. But they'll expect you to magically read their mind. We've seen this play out many times. Especially, let me be honest, with **Marwari families**. 90% of the time. They'll give you a brief that's random, but instead of admitting it, they'll push you to "just start." And then they'll reject everything later.

At this point, you need to step in and ask for references. Get pictures. Pin down the direction.

And yes, sometimes they'll ask for out-of-the-box things.
Like, "Helicopter se entry chahiye, Zubair bhai."
On a ground where there's live electric wiring on both sides.

That's when you have to put your foot down and say, "Boss, this is not going to happen."

And if that "no" means you lose the client? Then let them go.

Because that one "yes" can become a full-blown disaster later.

I'd rather lose a confused client than lose my sleep.

IMPORTANCE OF A WEDDING THEME (IN CRISP BEFORE WE DISCUSS AHEAD):

- **Cohesion:**
  A well-defined theme creates a unified look and feel throughout the wedding, ensuring all elements are harmonious.
- **Personalization:**
  A theme allows the couple to infuse their personalities and story into the wedding, making it unique and memorable.
- **Guidance:**
  A theme provides direction for decision-making regarding decor, attire, and other wedding details, simplifying the planning process.
- **Aesthetic Appeal:**
  A consistent theme enhances the visual appeal of the event, creating a more immersive and enjoyable experience for guests.
- **Memorability:**
  A distinct theme makes the wedding stand out, leaving a lasting impression on guests.

| 17 |

Tips for Choosing a Theme & Color Palette

Match the Theme to the Space, Not the Other Way Around

Let's start with the basics.

When someone says they want a boho-themed *Haldi,* you know what works, right? Sunlight, earthy textures, florals, vibrant drapes, and natural elements. That kind of setup looks gorgeous in an outdoor setting.

But what if the only option is an indoor banquet?

You don't cancel the theme. You shift focus to the lighting. You figure out how to bring that soft glow, that airiness, that open-feel *vibe,* even in a closed space. That's your job as a planner.

What Most Venues Get Wrong

You walk into a venue and see blue lights on the ceiling. Or red. I've seen venues spend crores on marble and mirror work and then leave the ugliest ceiling lights switched on the entire time.

Rule one: turn them off.

Especially for events like *Sangeet,* you don't need house lights. You need your lighting. House lights for a *Sangeet* make zero sense. 99% of the time, we switch them off and run our own rig.

For an outdoor *Sangeet*, you've got moonlight to deal with. But even there, your setup, LEDs, string lights, and focused beams can control the experience.

When the Spotlight Makes a Statement

Let me give you an example from one of our big weddings.

We were in a massive ballroom. For the evening function, we rigged up the ceiling with truss, and we focused spotlights only on the family table and the speaker on stage. That's it.

The rest of the hall was almost dark. Imagine the visual: everyone in a soft haze, and one table glowing in light. It made the family feel seen.

Whether it's the grandparents, the bride's mama, or the bride and groom themselves, that moment stays with them forever. That's memory-making.

But Can You Afford That Mood?

Of course, it depends on the budget. Spotlights, ceiling structure, custom lighting elements, they come at a cost. But when you have the budget, use it wisely. It's not about how much you spend. It's about how it makes people feel.

| 18 |

Incorporating Client Personalities & Preferences

Personalisation: Start with Listening

Next comes personalisation.

The biggest mistake planners make is that they pitch too fast. So, slow down, ask and then listen. It's about understanding what the family actually wants, how they feel, and what matters to them.

Let the bride or groom speak. Let the parents share stories. Then suggest themes, colors, elements that match their energy, not yours.

Sometimes you can take something small and make it stand out.

We had this birthday event with just 50 people. (Yes, not a wedding but still a good learning).

I got each guest's name printed on edible sheets and placed on cupcakes.

Simple idea. But it worked. You wouldn't expect what happened. People went nuts. They clicked photos. Posted on stories. Everyone loved it.

Big Budgets, Small Budgets. Same Stress, Different Shape

People think planning a wedding is easier when there's money. It's not.

I've worked on weddings where the budget was so high, you could buy a 3BHK in Indiranagar with it. And I've also worked on weddings where the family wanted a designer setup with a budget that wouldn't even cover the snacks at a *Mehendi*.

Both test you.

Let's talk about extremes in detail.

On one side, you've got those massive, high-profile weddings where nothing is impossible, except... we'll discuss.

On the other, you've got tight-budget weddings, where you're expected to pull off Pinterest-level setups with what's basically a pocketful of change.

Both come with their own headaches. And as a planner, you need to know how to navigate both without losing your sanity.

In big-budget weddings, the demands aren't just high; they're *high, urgent, and specific.*

They can say, "We want flowers from Holland." Seems doable when you have one month before the event. But what if there are only 7 days left? Then it becomes a game of luck. Sometimes we get it done. Sometimes it's just not humanly possible.

That's the stress with high-budget weddings. Not the money, but the expectations vs. timeline. Because the assumption is: "We're paying. You figure it out."

And trust me, I've had to "figure it out" in three different time zones on the same day. It's not as glamorous as it looks.

Now flip the coin.

A client comes to you and says, "Zubair bhai, *full sunflower decor chahiye*. The budget is Rupees 50,000." (We want a complete sunflower décor).

Real sunflowers across an entire venue? Not possible in that budget. So what do I do? I call up my decorator.

"Check the godown. Do we have artificial sunflowers?"

Maybe we rent some. Maybe we create a custom print. Maybe we work with lighting and color tones to *simulate* the feel.

That's where experience kicks in.

In low-budget weddings, your job is to take their vision and reimagine it through the lens of resources. No complaining. You study what's already available in your network. You rework the layout. You blend what's real with what's styled. And somehow, by the end of it, they are left in awe.

Whether the budget is Rupees 5 lakhs or Rupees 5 crores, the family wants the same thing: a wedding to remember. They want their guests to be happy. They want the bride and groom to feel special. They want moments. So don't treat the budget as your north star. Treat it as your starting point.

And then, based on that, you figure out whether you're flying flowers from Europe or not.

Walk Into the Room Prepared or Don't Walk In at All

We'd hired a digital marketing agency a while back. Six months in and there were no results. So I fired them. Gave a new agency a chance because the founder was a friend of my cousin.

I set up a meeting. The guy shows up empty-handed. No report. I ended that meeting in one and a half minutes. Said: "Come back with the data. Until then, we're not discussing anything."

Why? Because if you can't even come with your own report, how do you expect me to trust you with my brand?

And that same rule applies to weddings.

If you come to me and say, *"Let's talk about theme ideas,"* but don't have a single reference, mood board, or thought-through plan, **you're wasting everyone's time**.

You might think, *"Let's just see how the conversation flows."* Bad idea. Take it in writing, the client's going to start asking you real questions

"What kind of themes do you recommend for this venue?"

"Do you have visuals for a disco-style *Sangeet?*"

"Can you do pastels without making it look cliché?"

And you'll be sitting there without a word in. That's the moment the client decides, *"this one's not ready."*

Especially if you're new in the industry, don't expect confidence to magically show up in the meeting. You build it before the meeting. By doing the one thing most people skip. ACTUALLY PREPARING.

You don't need years of experience to impress someone. You need:

- Visuals
- Ready-made mood boards
- Clear understanding of what works and why

If you walk in with those three things, you've already won half the battle. If you don't? You're depending on luck and vague generalities. And trust me, *clients can smell that from a mile away.*

You Have AI Now. Use It.

There are no excuses anymore. You've got tools like ChatGPT, Midjourney, Canva. You can generate 20–25 complete mood boards in a day, across all types of wedding themes.

I did this a year ago. Built my core deck of wedding themes. Now, in my first meeting, before the client even opens their mouth, I show them a spread and say:

"This is what I've built. Take a look. Tell me what you like."

And just like that, I have the lead. The clients will stop questioning your experience.

You just need to **do it once, properly**.

Update it once in a while. Add fresh references as trends evolve. The client doesn't ask if you're experienced. They think, "They know what they are doing."

And that's the kind of impression & trust that no logo or tagline can buy you.

Pretty Is Fine. But What Experience Are You Creating?

Look, today's crowd has seen beautiful weddings. They've been to Pinterest-inspired *haldis*, floral tunnels, and fairy-lit receptions.

What they're chasing now? **Something new.**

Let me tell you what we did for a **Bollywood night** *sangeet*. Every person in India has at least heard of Bollywood night *sangeet*, if not attended. But we asked ourselves: What can we do differently?

Now earlier, Bollywood themes were all about retro songs and old film posters. That's still fine, but today's generation is living in the world of Instagram and paparazzi culture.

As guests walked into the venue, we had **paparazzi-style lights flashing**, a faux press wall setup, and a team clicking pictures like it was a red-carpet entry.

The moment they entered, they **felt like celebrities**. They asked for a Bollywood night, we gave them a Bollywood night with a Page 3 experience.

And that—*that*—is the difference between planning a theme and **orchestrating a moment**.

Not Every Theme Will Make Sense to You. It Doesn't Have to.

Let me tell you why 90% of wedding planners don't make it past a few years. They go into every wedding thinking, *"How do I make this look good on my Instagram?"* And in doing that, they completely ignore the client's story.

Big mistake. If the bride says no to your favourite design, it's not personal. It's a preference.

And in that moment, you don't argue with their taste. You respect the sentiment, and you build around it.

Because the job is not to make it *your kind of wedding*. The job is to make it *their kind of wedding*.

Most planners fail because they don't listen. You can't force your creative vision on someone who didn't ask for it. The moment you start doing that, everything goes off track.

The best themes I've built came from conversations.

I've had clients ask for setups that made no visual sense. What I realised was that it was about emotion. Maybe it's how the bride grew up. Maybe it's a tribute to a family story. Maybe it's a memory they're emotionally attached to.

I listened. I picked up on the emotion behind what they were saying. I ignored what I personally liked and focused on what they personally needed. And that's what made the wedding unforgettable for them.

So next time you build a theme, ask yourself:

Am I designing something beautiful?

Or am I designing something that will **mean something** to them?

If it's both, you've nailed it.

MODULE 6

VENDOR SELECTION

"A wedding planner is the hand that fixes the bow before anyone sees the knot."-**Unknown**

| 19 |

The Vendors That Make or Break Your Wedding

A wedding is only as good as the people you bring on board. Over the years, I've worked with all kinds of vendors — some who became family, and some I'd never work with again. In this chapter, I'll walk you through the key vendors you'll need to work with and what to look for in each one.

But first, here's a quick snapshot of the major players involved:

- **Caterers:**
  - Provide food and beverage services for the wedding reception and other events.
  - Offer options like plated dinners, buffets, or food stations.
- **Florists:**
  - Design and create floral arrangements, including bouquets, centerpieces, and decorative installations.
  - Provide advice on seasonal flowers and design trends.
- **Photographers:**
  - Capture moments from the wedding day through professional photography.
  - Offer different packages, including engagement shoots, wedding albums, and digital images.

- **Videographers:**
    - Create a video recording of the wedding day.
    - Offer services like highlight reels, full-length videos, and same-day edits.
- **Venue:**
    - Provide the location for the ceremony and reception.
    - May include services such as setup, cleanup, and coordination.
- **Entertainment:**
    - Includes DJs, live bands, or musicians for ceremony and reception music.
    - Provide sound and lighting equipment as needed.
- **Bakers:**
    - Design and create the wedding cake and other desserts.
    - Offer tastings and custom cake designs.
- **Attire:**
    - Bridal shops and tailors provide wedding dresses, suits, and accessories.
    - Offer alteration services to ensure a perfect fit.
- **Transportation:**
    - Provide vehicles for the wedding party and guests, such as limousines, buses, or vintage cars.
    - Ensure timely arrival and departure from venues.
- **Hair and Makeup Artists:**
    - Provide beauty services for the bride, groom, and wedding party.
    - Offer trials to determine the desired look.
- **Stationery:**
    - Design and print invitations, save-the-dates, programs, and thank-you cards.
    - Offer custom designs and coordination with the wedding theme.
- **Rentals:**
    - Provide items like tents, tables, chairs, linens, and decor.

    ◦ Ensure delivery, setup, and teardown services.

Now that you've got a grip on the roles, we'll go deeper into what really matters

Seasonal Florals: Know What Grows Where and When

First things first, you need to know what flowers are in season.

Every city, every month has its own floral reality. If you're planning a wedding in December in Delhi, don't start dreaming about tulips unless you know how to source them—or how to replace them.

Even for smaller budget weddings, seasonal planning is everything.

You should always be aware of:

- What's locally available in that city
- What's affordable in that month
- And how long it lasts once it's cut

Now, in high-budget weddings, yes, flowers can be flown in from anywhere in the country. But even then, **logistics are tricky**.

Let's say you're getting rajnigandha from Bangalore to Kolkata. You need to know:

- When it's harvested
- How long it takes to ship
- How fresh it will be on arrival

Because if it's cut two days before and shipped without proper care, it'll arrive wilted. No one wants a droopy *Mandap*.

Another detail people miss is lifespan.

If your setup needs to hold for three days and the client insists on only real flowers, you need to:

- Choose the right flowers

- Know how to store and water them
- Plan floral layering accordingly

We've spoken about mood boards already. But it is essential to carry color swatches and fabric samples to client meetings.

This helps you lock decisions faster. Now the question is where do you get these swatches and samples from. Reach out to your decorators and vendors and request a swatch book, a small kit with key colors, fabrics, and material textures. Keep it in your meeting bag. The moment you say, *"Here's the actual fabric we're thinking of,"* you've already earned credibility.

When It Comes to Florists, Sampling is Everything.

A florist can send you beautiful videos and photos, but they may not be theirs. Or they may be from a different scale of work. So, always ask for **a live sampling**.

"Show me how this looks on a real scale."

"Let me see how you style this centerpiece."

"Let's test it under the lighting we're using."

The craftsmanship of *karigars* impacts how beautiful & exquisite your floral decor would look. You can hire the best decorator in the business. But if their *karigars* aren't skilled, the setup will look average at best.

When you're just starting out, you might not know how to assess this.

So spend time with the vendors. Visit their warehouses. Watch their team work. Ask for live demos.

Your real quality control lies in the last pair of hands that touch the work.

When the Decor Was So Grand... No One Noticed the Bride

We were handling decor for a wedding where the client had gone **all-in on grandeur**, huge budget, oversized setups, massive floral installations, chandeliers, layered textures, the works.

We were brought in just for the decor. The wedding planner was someone else. We were at the venue, and the *pheras* were supposed to start soon. Suddenly, we noticed a woman sitting quietly on the *Mandap.*

And I kid you not! For 10 whole minutes, none of us on-ground knew she was the **bride.**

She had minimal makeup. There was no planned entry, no lighting highlight, nothing to say *"here comes the bride."* She just... appeared.

We actually thought she was one of the guests. Until someone whispered, *"That's the bride"*. I was shocked.

The decor was so overpowering that the bride got lost in it. And when I say "lost," I mean quite literally invisible. Now, don't get me wrong, she may have wanted it that way – simple and understated. But that's exactly the point.

If the bride wants to stay low-key, your decor should support that. Not overpower it.

There has to be a balance. There has to be alignment between the decor design and the main characters of the day.

Because no one's coming to a wedding to see your chandeliers. They're coming to see the bride and groom. And when they become background characters in their own wedding, you've failed.

If You Didn't Capture It, It Never Happened

Look, I'll say this without sugarcoating it. **If you're not capturing your work properly, you're doing injustice to yourself.**

When you're new in the industry, don't think twice about hiring a solid photographer *for yourself.*

Yes, I said for yourself, not just for the client.

Because while they're capturing the bride walking in and the father tearing up, you need someone capturing:

- Your team setting up at 3 AM
- The floral ceiling being raised

- The before/after of a ballroom that looked like a factory and turned into a dream

What's special about these moments is that they are already happening. You just need someone to capture them.

That's your credibility. That's what makes people trust you before they even call you. And that's what makes people trust you even after they call you.

Client Shoots vs. Content Shoots: Know the Difference

Photography planning has two sides.

1. The client's requirement

If it's a small wedding, one photographer + one videographer might do.

But for a larger wedding, you're looking at:

- 1 candid photographer
- 1 candid videographer
- 1 traditional photo team
- 1 traditional video team

And sometimes even more. For big moments, we've had:

- 1 close-up camera
- 1 wide-angle lens camera

All aimed at the same scene. Because that's how you get those cinematic wedding films people are obsessed with nowadays.

The Horror Stories No One Talks About

I've had clients who booked their photographers, and then they've come to me crying...literally crying...because it's been a year, and they still haven't received their wedding footage.

They haven't even gotten the full video. Some have had to wait until their first anniversary. Some never got them at all. Why? Because the vendor lost the footage, or delayed it, or just vanished.

The "Where's the *Haar*?" Incident

Let me tell you about one wedding that still makes me laugh... and panic a little.

It was a Muslim wedding. Now, Muslim weddings don't have *vermala* ritual (traditionally). But sometimes this ritual is included, if the family wants to do it.

However, in one particular wedding, the family didn't mention *vermala* at all. So we assumed there were no garlands needed.

On the wedding day, just before the ceremony, someone runs up to me and says: *"Zubair bhai, where's the haar?"*

I said, "What *haar?* The gold shopping has been done by your own family, so which *haar* do you mean?" They said, "No! The floral one, the wedding garland!"

I said, "Nobody told us you needed a *haar!*"

They said, "But we thought you'd arrange it."

So now my people are racing to arrange a garland in the final moments 2 hours before the ceremony. No heads-up. No mention in the brief. But you do what you have to do.

That day taught me something I carry into every wedding now: **Never assume the client will tell you everything.** Most of the time, they don't even know what they've forgotten.

So it's your job to come with your own checklist. Ask about:

- Ritual items
- Specific entry moments
- Cultural expectations
- Who's handling what
- What's assumed and what's confirmed

Because you're not just the planner. You're the only one asking the questions no one else thought to ask.

So... Are There Vendors for Venues?

Short answer: yes.

Long answer: you better find out before you take the booking.

Some venues come with clauses, like:

"Sound and lighting must be done through our in-house vendor."

"Night décor? Only our empanelled decorator can do it."

If you want the venue, then you work with their guy. The venue's making a cut. Simple.

So always ask who's locked in before you're locked in.

Outfits and themes! Who's responsible?

Sometimes the client wants you to be involved in the outfit. Sometimes they don't. And often, it's because they think you're making money off it. That's okay. Everybody's preferences differ.

But did I tell you the surprises an attire can hold for your event? Here's one...

Three days before the wedding, the bride told us she's changed her mind. She's got herself a deep red *Sabyasachi lehenga* tailored in custom size. And now she expected us to tweak the decor to match her *lehenga.*

We were working with a completely different colour palette. Everything was set. But that's how this goes.

We didn't argue. We added red elements where we could. Rebalanced the look. Did enough so that the *lehenga* didn't feel out of place.

That's the job sometimes. You make last-minute changes look like part of the plan.

Transportation

Transport is where it all begins. If it's a destination wedding and your guests are flying in, that airport-to-hotel experience is the first thing they're going to feel. If that goes wrong, the wedding starts off on the wrong foot.

At one wedding (yep, the same one where we didn't get paid), the client wanted a full custom makeup room. We set up a whole salon experience for the bride and groom's family.

You can't just throw whatever chairs the venue gives you.

If the client doesn't have the budget to rent fresh inventory, your job is to look at what's available and design around it.

Tablecloths, chair backs, runners, all of it should sync with the theme. It's a small detail, but casts a big impact.

With vendors, always get multiple quotes. Always compare work. And never choose the cheapest, thinking you've found a hack, because if it's cheap, it's cheap for a reason.

Build a relationship, but also: don't get too emotionally attached to your vendors. I've had vendors I've worked with for years... who still dropped the ball.

The *Sangeet* Disaster That Cost Us Rupees 7–8 Lakhs

Let me tell you what happened. There was planning, and then there's *what actually happens on the ground.*

It was a big *Sangeet.* High-profile.

We had a vendor handling sound and light. The band had a tech rider, specific sound requirements, and equipment.

We'd sent the tech rider to the vendor. But my team never discussed it. The vendor assumed it was for the DJ, not the live band. So they didn't bring the required setup.

The band arrived at 5 PM. The event was set to start at 7 PM. No tech. No time. The band couldn't perform.

It wasn't even our fault directly. We had shared the Excel, we had done the handover, but we didn't discuss it. Well, the client was furious and quite rightly so. And it cost us close to Rupees 8 lakhs in payments that were withheld.

Just sending a tech rider or list over email or WhatsApp isn't enough. You must walk the vendor through every single line. Especially if you trust them. Because when you get too comfortable, that's when details get missed.

Now we've made it a rule: no tech rider goes un-reviewed. And yes, even if you've worked with someone for years, you still double-check.

Should There Be Backup Plans for Trusted Vendors? Always.

Even your go-to vendor might get sick. Their team might bail. They might show up underprepared. So always have a backup vendor for every major service. Because if things collapse, no one's asking your vendors "why".

They're asking *you.*

| 20 |

How to Find & Choose Reliable Vendors

Research

Start by checking everything. Use wedding directories, social media, and Google reviews. But don't stop there. Look for reviews where clients have talked about **after-service**, timelines, and how they handled stress. That tells you what you need to know.

Recommendations

As we've already discussed earlier, **referrals matter.** Talk to fellow planners, decorators, or past clients. If someone's worked with the same vendor more than once, there's a reason.

Interviews and Meetings

I never book a vendor without sitting across the table (or screen) and having a real conversation. Ask about:

- Their past work
- How many events they've handled like yours
- What happens if something goes wrong

More than the answers, watch how they respond. If they get defensive, you already know.

Portfolios and Samples

Ask for unfiltered footage, setup videos, BTS from weddings. As we discussed in the previous chapter, sampling matters. You want to see how florists style live, not just what they pulled from Pinterest. Same goes for stationery, cakes, draping – always ask for a real sample, and witness their work.

References

This is one of the most ignored steps. People get impressed by big names and forget to dig deeper. Call up their last 2-3 clients. Ask:

- How was their communication?
- Were they punctual?
- Did they stay within budget?
- Were there any surprises?

And if a vendor refuses to share references, that's a "no" from me.

Contracts and Pricing

As we've discussed earlier in the contracts module, never rely on verbal promises. Write it all down. Cross-check what's included, what's not, and the cancellation/refund policy.

Especially for big-ticket vendors like sound & light, photographers, and decorators, read the tech riders, line items, and breakdown of responsibilities.

And yes, cheap doesn't mean cost-effective. Sometimes, you'll pay less upfront and bleed on event day. So choose wisely.

I cannot stress this enough. Always have a Plan B. Even if you trust your vendor blindly, have a backup ready. Because on the wedding day, you don't get second chances.

| 21 |

Building a Good Relationship with Vendors

If you stay in this business long enough, you'll realise something: your vendors are your last-minute saviours. You build great relationships with them in a non-negotiable part of the trade. And here's how:

Clear Communication:

This one's a no-brainer but so many people still get it wrong. You've got to be clear from Day 1. Whether it's your vision, the scope of work, timelines, or specific deliverables, spell everything out. Call. Talk. Reconfirm.

(As we already discussed in the tech rider fiasco, never skip the discussion part, even with trusted vendors.)

Respect and Professionalism:

Even if they're your friends, treat them like professionals. Respect their expertise. You may know your client well, but your vendor probably knows the venue better. Listen. Take suggestions. This isn't about ego.

Timely Responses:

If they need approvals, don't keep them waiting. If they're asking for payment release as per the contract, make sure it's ready. Because your delay creates a domino effect across everything they've planned.

Collaboration:

Vendors are not order-takers. Be open to their input. Let them be part of the creative problem-solving process. When things go wrong (and they often will), you'll be glad you made them feel like a partner, not a vendor.

Appreciation:

I've said this in team meetings a hundred times: don't just give feedback when something goes wrong. If something was on point, the floral work, the lighting, the way they handled a guest - say it. Share it. Maybe even post about it. It goes a long way in creating loyalty. And loyalty goes a long way when you need a favour at the 11th hour.

Follow-Up:

The wedding is done. The family has left. But your relationship with the vendor shouldn't end there. Drop them a message. Thank them personally. Ask how their experience was working with your team.

If they trust you, they'll show up for you. Every time.

Remember, great vendors make you look good. And that only happens when the people behind the scenes are respected, appreciated, and trusted to do their best work.

MODULE 7

TIMELINE & CHECKLIST

"A well-planned wedding isn't about having endless time—it's about making every minute count. Whether you have a year or a month, the secret is in the checklist, not the clock."-**Unknown**

| 22 |

Mastering the Wedding Timeline

So... How Early Should You Start?

Ideally, six months in advance is solid. Twelve months is a luxury. We've pulled off weddings in three months, two months, even **one month**.

So if you're reading this thinking *"I only have 5 months left,"* relax. You can still pull it off.

Just know that the shorter the runway, the tighter your planning has to be.

Create a checklist and share it with every vendor. And I mean a real copy, not a WhatsApp forward.

- When is the material arriving?
- When is the setup happening?
- When does it need to be ready?
- When does teardown begin?

Your sheet should answer all of that. If your setup is ready 10 minutes before the event, you're late. You aim to be done at least an hour before the guests arrive.

That's the window where everything should look effortless, even if it wasn't.

| 23 |

Creating A Wedding Planning Timeline

If you ask me what truly separates a seamless wedding from a stressful one, it's this right here.

This planning timeline is mine and it can be your event-day Bible.

12+ Months Before:

- **Engagement Announcement:** Share the news with family and friends.
- **Budget:** Set a realistic budget.
- **Guest List:** Start drafting the guest list.
- **Venue:** Research and book the venue.
- **Wedding Planner:** Hire a wedding planner if desired.

9–12 Months Before:

- **Save the Dates:** Send out save-the-date cards.
- **Vendors:** Book key vendors (caterer, photographer, videographer, entertainment, florist).
- **Dress Shopping:** Begin shopping for the wedding dress and attire for the wedding party.
- **Engagement Photos:** Schedule and take engagement photos.

6–9 Months Before:

- **Design and Decor:** Start planning the theme, decor, and color palette.
- **Invitations:** Choose and order wedding invitations.
- **Registry:** Set up a wedding registry.
- **Accommodation:** Reserve a block of hotel rooms for out-of-town guests.
- **Tasting:** Schedule tastings with the caterer and baker.

4–6 Months Before:

- **Finalize Guest List:** Confirm the guest list and send out invitations.
- **Attire:** Finalize wedding dress and attire for the wedding party.
- **Transportation:** Book transportation for the wedding day.
- **Music and Entertainment:** Finalize song lists and entertainment details.
- **Hair and Makeup:** Book hair and makeup artists and schedule trials.

2–4 Months Before:

- **Rehearsal Dinner:** Plan and book the rehearsal dinner.
- **Ceremony Details:** Finalize ceremony details and officiant.
- **Marriage License:** Apply for a marriage license.
- **Favors and Gifts:** Purchase or create wedding favors and gifts for the wedding party.

1–2 Months Before:

- **Final Fittings:** Schedule final fittings for wedding attire.
- **Seating Chart:** Create the seating chart.

- **Confirm Vendors:** Confirm all vendor arrangements and provide final headcounts.
- **Timeline:** Create a detailed wedding day timeline.

2–4 Weeks Before:

- **Follow-Up:** Confirm arrival times and details with all vendors.
- **Packing:** Pack for the honeymoon.
- **Final Payments:** Make final payments to vendors.

1 Week Before:

- **Rehearsal:** Conduct the wedding rehearsal.
- **Emergency Kit:** Prepare a wedding day emergency kit (sewing kit, stain remover, etc.).

Wedding Day:

- **Relax:** Enjoy the day and focus on the celebration.

Important Milestones and Deadlines:

- **12 Months Before:** Book venue, set budget, draft guest list.
- **9 Months Before:** Hire vendors, send save-the-dates, start dress shopping.
- **6 Months Before:** Finalize decor, order invitations, set up registry.
- **4 Months Before:** Send invitations, book transportation, finalize music.
- **2 Months Before:** Plan rehearsal dinner, apply for marriage license.
- **1 Month Before:** Confirm vendors, finalize seating chart, create timeline.
- **1 Week Before:** Conduct rehearsal, prepare emergency kit.

| 24 |

Day of Wedding Checklist

Morning:

- **Bride and Groom:** Ensure both have a good breakfast and stay hydrated.
- **Attire:** Check that all attire is ready and steamed/pressed if needed.
- **Hair and Makeup:** Confirm hair and makeup artists' arrival times.
- **Emergency Kit:** Have the emergency kit on hand.

Before the Ceremony:

- **Vendors:** Confirm all vendors have arrived and are setting up as planned.
- **Decor:** Check that all decor is in place according to the plan.
- **Photographer:** Ensure the photographer captures pre-ceremony moments.
- **Transportation:** Confirm transportation arrangements for the wedding party.

Ceremony:

- **Programs:** Ensure wedding programs are distributed.

- **Music:** Confirm ceremony music is set up and ready.
- **Officiant:** Check in with the officiant and ensure they have the necessary documents.

Reception:

- **Seating:** Confirm seating arrangements are as planned.
- **Dinner:** Ensure the caterer is ready for dinner service.
- **Speeches:** Confirm the order and timing of speeches and toasts.
- **Entertainment:** Ensure the DJ or band is ready and has the music list.

Throughout the Day:

- **Timeline:** Follow the detailed wedding day timeline to ensure everything runs smoothly.
- **Point of Contact:** Have a designated person (wedding planner or trusted friend) to handle any issues.
- **Enjoy:** Remember to enjoy the day and take moments to savor the celebration.

Now that we've built everything block by block, let's talk about pulling it all down. Because what you *don't* plan to dismantle properly... can dismantle your reputation.

The Dismantling Disaster That Got a Vendor Banned

This happened with a friend of mine.

He completed the event beautifully. But once the event ended, they got busy with another function and forgot to dismantle their setup on time.

The venue had another wedding the next morning. And because the previous decor team didn't clear the space in time, the new wedding got delayed. Big-time. The venue had to compensate the next client. Money was lost.

And guess what the venue did? **They banned my friend from organising any events in the future, permanently.**

This wasn't a small-time decorator either. This was a reputed event manager. But one misstep, and his name was off the list.

These are the kind of lessons you learn from other people's mistakes. Teardown time is just as important as setup time.

Now, in every vendor briefing, we ask:

- "How long will the teardown take?"
- "What's your earliest dismantle slot?"
- "Do you have a dedicated dismantle team?"

And of course, we ask the venue as well: how long can we get for dismantling? We also mark it clearly on the timeline sheet:

"Dismantle begins at X time. Must be cleared by Y."

You don't want to get that 2 AM call saying the venue is pissed because the carpets are still lying around.

Booking the Venue Early: Not Everyone Does It. But Smart Clients Do.

Most Indian clients don't book venues a year in advance. But then... you meet the outliers. Like this one client from the US who called me in December 2023 to discuss a wedding for December 2026.

Yes. Three years ahead.

He wanted the venue locked right now. Because for him, it's normal. That's how it's done back there. You may not always get this kind of lead time, but if you do, grab it. You'll get better pricing, better availability, and a lot less stress.

Wedding Day Logistics? Set Boundaries Early.

Now let's come to day-of transport logistics. This is where things get messy, guests start asking for custom drop-offs, side trips, and city tours. So, before the big day, sit with the client and ask:

"Do you want to allow your guests to go anywhere they want? Or should we limit it to planned pickups/drops only?"

If the client says *"Let them go wherever they want"*, cool. Just make sure it's communicated clearly to the logistics team.

If not, then this is how you handle the guests: Tell them, "This ride is chargeable."

Say it politely but firmly. It avoids drama and protects your time.

Emergency Kits: The Stuff That Saves You at 9 AM After a 3 AM *Sangeet*

Weddings are messy. People overeat. People drink. And then they have *Haldi* at 9 AM the next morning. You want to know what makes a guest feel taken care of? A small kit with:

- Water
- Mints
- Headache tablets
- Lip balm
- Energy bar
- And yes...**a hangover kit**

We once made **250 hangover kits** for a wedding and dropped it in each room. That one kit got more praise from the groom than the main event guy. Because no one else thought of it.

When I had pitched the idea of hangover kits, I vividly recall the groom taking me aside later to remark: You're far better than the guy we've hired for the job.

If you've made it this far in the book, the day isn't far when you will hear many praises & attract events based on your reputation.

MODULE 8

MANAGING THE WEDDING DAY

"A wedding isn't magic—it's math. 80% planning, 20% execution. 100% accountability. Miss one number, and the equation collapses."- ***Zubair Abdul Waheed***

| 25 |

Preparing for The Wedding Day

Thousands of weddings across countries, cities, and cultures later, what can an event manager tell you? We've said this before, and I'll say it again here:

80% of wedding management is planning. Only 20% is execution. Yet, on the day of the wedding, delegate 80% of the work, and keep no more than 20% of coordination or management on your shoulders.

Quickly running through the essentials of preparing for the wedding day, make sure you cover these in advance:

- **Create a Detailed Timeline:**
    - Develop a comprehensive schedule that outlines every event and activity for the wedding day, from getting ready to the reception's end.
    - Include specific times for vendor arrivals, setup, ceremony, cocktail hour, dinner, speeches, dances, and other key moments.
- **Confirm with Vendors:**
    - Reach out to all vendors one week before the wedding to confirm final details, arrival times, and services.
    - Provide each vendor with a copy of the wedding day timeline.
- **Prepare Emergency Kits:**

- Assemble emergency kits for both the bride and groom, including items like sewing kits, stain remover, pain relievers, snacks, water, and extra makeup.

- **Delegate Responsibilities:**
  - Assign specific tasks to reliable friends, family members, or the wedding party to ensure all aspects are covered.
  - Consider hiring a day-of coordinator to manage logistics and handle any last-minute issues.
- **Pack Essentials:**
  - Ensure all necessary items for the wedding day are packed and ready, such as attire, accessories, marriage license, rings, and personal items.
- **Rehearse:**
  - Conduct a wedding rehearsal with the bridal party and officiant to practice the ceremony's flow and iron out any potential issues.

Strategy People vs. Execution People

This is something I wish more planning teams took seriously. You need two types of people on your wedding crew: **strategic managers** and **execution managers**.

Strategic people can see the full picture. They know how to map timelines, preempt risks, handle vendors calmly, and think on their feet. They are your "why is this happening and how do we fix it" people.

Execution people are your doers. You give them a task and it's done. No questions, no ego, no delay. Need all the guest chairs adjusted? It gets handled. Need to get the bride's luggage from one villa to another? It gets done. But don't expect them to walk into a family meeting or redesign a flow last minute.

The mistake most planners make is that they confuse the two. They give thinking work to doers and doing work to thinkers. And then everything starts slipping out of hand at the same time.

Two Managers. Two Very Different Roles.

You need:

1. A Production Manager: someone who ensures the vendors are showing up on time, materials are coming in, setups are getting built, and the full decor is coming together as planned. When I say production, I include decor. This person is your pre-event manager.
2. A Show Manager: someone who takes over once everything is set. This person handles the sound check, artist entries, guest movement, lighting, and flow of the show. This is your in-event manager.

They're not interchangeable. They may overlap, but the energy and focus needed are very different. Event to event, these roles might rotate. But you need both minds present.

When to Hire Them?

Ideally, you get them on board as soon as the wedding is confirmed. The earlier you onboard them, the smoother your planning becomes.

But, if the budget doesn't allow for a long engagement, you bring them in at least one to two weeks before the event. Minimum.

And when you do, you need to:

- Give them a full download of the event
- Introduce them to all vendors
- Walk them through the timeline
- Add them to the WhatsApp coordination group
- Get them aligned with the flow

Once they're looped in, you can stop micromanaging.

How Much Do They Charge?

I've worked with managers who've charged:

- Rupees 2,000 per day
- Rupees 25,000 per day

Both types exist. Who you need to hire depends on experience, capacity, and the kind of event. Some of my friends have called and said,

"Zubair, I just need you to come and manage the whole thing. Everything is falling into chaos. Tell me your price."

I've quoted Rupees 3-4 lakhs for being present for 2 days and managing a full-scale wedding. Now, of course, I didn't handle the entire wedding alone. In fact, I brought in two senior people from my team. I just came in, reviewed the flow, slept, woke up, checked once more, and that was it.

You don't need to be in ten places to deliver a memorable wedding.

For the Decor Manager: When Do They Exit?

Your production/decor manager usually wraps up when the setup is done and live show cues begin. That's when the show manager steps in on D-Day. He is the one handling tech riders, sound checks, artist timing, scripting cues, etc.

But ideally, even the show manager is looped in two days prior, so they can:

- Walk the venue
- Review the sound and lighting specs
- Get vendor clarity
- Double-check what's promised vs. what's been delivered

Because if the planner doesn't know how many par cans, truss lights, or mic channels are needed, what are you managing? And this book won't teach you what to book. THAT you'll learn by doing.

Timelines Are for Survival.

A timeline is your reality check. It tells you when vendors arrive, when each material lands, when rehearsals happen, when transport is scheduled, and, this part people always forget, when you need to exit the venue.

At one wedding, the event ended at 3 AM. The hotel said we had to vacate the entire setup by 7 AM. Four hours. Now remember, that same setup had taken us **12 hours to build**.

So, how do you take down something in 4 hrs when it took you 12 hrs to build? The challenge is that you cannot break or tear down materials, because these are supposed to be returned to the godown (a non-negotiable for the profits we make).

We told the client, this kind of turnaround means we need extra labour. And we charged accordingly. We broke the teardown into zones:

- One team handled florals
- One took care of structural dismantling
- Another broke down the stage

Everyone had a task. And we were out by 6:45 AM.

Had we not done that, we would've delayed the next wedding at the venue, gotten a warning from the property, and probably lost a chunk of our inventory due to damage costing real money.

A lot of planners don't plan the teardown. But teardown is just as critical.

If your labour isn't briefed, or you don't have enough hands on deck, boys will just rip through the decor. They'll toss things around. And you'll end up with broken pillars, torn fabrics, and bent floral props.

All that material was your reusable inventory. If it's gone, your profit's gone.

There's a lot that goes into making a wedding feel smooth on the outside. But behind that seamless flow is a lot of invisible coordination. If you're not checking in with your vendors properly, not preparing the team for emergencies, or not assigning the right people to shadow the family, even the most beautiful wedding can fall apart.

One Week Before: Confirm, Repeat, Reconfirm

A week before the wedding, we reach out to every single vendor to confirm final details: their arrival time, service scope, and equipment load-in.

And no, we don't do this once. We run through the checklist multiple times. Sometimes vendors complain:

"You already told us this."

"Why are we repeating it?"

Because we've been burned before. Because we know how quickly a wedding day can spiral when one person is late or confused. And because this is the process. We follow it every time.

Timeline Sheets Are Not Optional

Every vendor gets a copy of the final wedding timeline. This is essential.

The structure vendor needs to know when the stage is being installed, so they can come right after. The floral team needs to know when the structure is up so they can step in.

If their florals are pre-arranged, they need to know where to stage them. If they're building on-site, they need to know the exact hour they'll get access.

In some cases, floral setup is done off-site and fixed on location. In others, it needs to be installed directly on the structure. That only works if each vendor knows their exact time window.

If everyone shows up at once, structure, florals, lights, band, logistics, you'll have a crowd with zero coordination. That's when people start tripping over each other, and delays begin.

Emergency Kits & Shadows: The Human Side of Planning

Emergency kits are not always mandatory; many families prepare their own. But we always recommend having a small, smart kit ready for the bride and groom. And we don't just keep it somewhere at the venue. We assign it to the shadows.

Who Are Shadows?

A shadow is a designated point of contact, someone placed with a key family member to make sure nothing slips through the cracks.

Every couple is assigned a shadow team, personal assistants for the bride, groom, and father who are more involved in managing the wedding. These shadows carry essentials in their bags: safety pins, mints, tissues, painkillers, makeup touch-up items, whatever might be needed in a pinch.

We make sure these shadows build rapport with the bride and groom before the wedding. You can't have a stranger fumbling around during a stressful moment. They need to feel like a friend, not a staff member.

Shadows Are Not Runners

Some families think the shadow is there to carry water bottles, shift furniture, and act like an extra hand.

"Bring this. Fetch that. Move this sofa. Hold this *lehenga* bag."

No. That's not their job. Shadows are there to ensure that your event doesn't fall apart due to miscommunication. They're human co-ordination points, not labour staff.

If you need manual support, hire labour. Don't treat a role meant for intelligent problem-solving like it's there for lifting suitcases.

Who Gets a Shadow?

Depends on the budget. In big weddings, we assign:

- One shadow for the bride
- One for the groom

- One each for both parents
- And sometimes even one for the siblings

But the most critical pairing is for the father of the bride or groom, especially when he's the one handling the logistics with the hotel.

In those cases, we assign **two shadows**:

1. A **hotel POC (Point of Contact)** who knows the venue, staff, and backend systems
2. An **event shadow** from our team who knows the family's needs, decor, and flow

They stick with him throughout. If he needs something from the hotel, the hotel POC gets it done. If he needs a change from our side, maybe a chair moved, or a car shifted, or a guest to be picked, our team handles it immediately.

This combination works beautifully in large-scale weddings, especially in five-star hotels or complete buyouts.

What a Shadow Actually Does

Let's say a shadow is assigned to the father of the bride.

Now, mid-event, someone walks up and says the *Mandap* lights are overheating or a path is blocked. The father doesn't need to panic or leave his guests.

The shadow listens, assesses, and communicates directly with the concerned team, decor, lighting, planning, whoever needs to fix it.

Sometimes, vendors or team members need to speak to the father. But instead of calling him directly, which we never do, we call the shadow.

We ask, "Is Sir free for a quick coordination call?"
If yes, it's done quietly. If not, the shadow manages it. That one layer of filtration saves time, dignity, and mental peace for everyone.

And If There's No Budget?

Not all clients want external shadow teams.

Sometimes they say, "We'll manage with our family. No need to hire extra people."

Fair enough. But in that case, **we assign roles clearly**.

- Who's handling guest transport?
- Who's speaking to the hotel?
- Who's monitoring vendor arrivals?
- Who's updating the planner when timelines shift?

If there's no professional team, then internal family members must be briefed like professionals. Otherwise, everyone gets tired, confused, and frustrated. We've seen this in the early years like 10 to 15 years ago, weddings ran on *mamas, chachas, and cousins*. Back then, planners were decorators. Now, decorators are part of the planning team. And planners run the show.

"This Is the Most Difficult Client I've Ever Handled"

There was a recent wedding. I have handled tough clients, and usually tough for others isn't tough for me. For this particular wedding, eventually, we weren't even paid, so yeah, tough all the way through.

I remember the hotel staff shadow, the guy told me straight up,

"Sir, I've done shadowing for so many clients. This one was the toughest in my entire career."

Later that night, the shadow of this client told he was facing troubles. When I asked him what happened, here's what we discovered. The client would say something one minute, then flip entirely in the next two minutes, and by the third minute, he'd ask,

"Why didn't you follow what I said the first time?"

If you tried to explain, he'd cut you off mid-sentence and say he didn't want excuses.

You couldn't reason with him. And I told the shadow,

"Next time, you need to keep a voice recorder running during conversations."

Not even joking. Play it back when he flips...

"Sir, this is what you said."

Because without proof, he'll turn around and pin the blame on you. The guy looked at me and said, *"I wish I had spoken to you earlier."*

The Walkthrough Rehearsal

When people don't know where to walk, what to do, or how the entry is supposed to happen, their face says, *"I don't know what I'm doing."* And at that moment, they have like seven cameras and fifty phones pointed at them.

It doesn't need two days of prep. But you do need a quick walkthrough with the bridal party, especially for the entries. Every member involved should know where they're coming from, where they stop, who moves when, and what cues are being followed.

We usually call everyone to do a dry run on the morning of the wedding.

Sangeet Rehearsals: Dry Runs, Props & Performers

For larger weddings where performances are involved, especially *Sangeet,* we make sure dry runs happen in advance.

While we're still finishing the stage setup, families often come in to check the stage, spacing, lighting levels. Many of them even do a quick practice then and there.

We usually try to keep the *Sangeet* venue ready by 5 PM, so they can come in, rehearse with their props, walk the stage, and feel confident.

Even the bride often comes in early, does a quick run-through before heading for hair and makeup.

The same applies for dancers, emcees, and anyone entering with a specific cue or choreography. These are not last-minute things you figure out during the function. You rehearse.

| 26 |

Managing The Wedding Day Schedule

You Can't Do Everything Yourself, But You Will Try When You're Starting Out

There's a point in every wedding planner's journey where you think you'll manage. And the truth is, you probably will. But you'll do it at the cost of sleep and your ability to breathe.

Because when you're starting out, you don't have a full team. You don't have department managers. You don't have a lineup of trained showrunners or coordinators. You've got you, a couple of freelancers if you're lucky, and a truckload of responsibilities.

On Wedding Day, We Always Assign a Showrunner

Once the day starts, everything has to follow the timeline. There's no "he's not ready yet, we'll adjust." If you give everyone that flexibility, the whole day will slip.

So we always assign a showrunner, someone who's responsible for running the timeline on ground. This is a person who:

- Knows the full flow of the event
- Has the timeline in hand
- Knows which vendors are doing what
- Can take calls if something shifts

- Is constantly checking if we're on time

They're the reason the varmala happens when it's supposed to, the dinner opens on time, and the DJ doesn't start before the lights cue in.

Besides showrunners, our team always assigns one manager per department. This manager is responsible for checking the arrival, setup, and checklist of their vendors.

But if you're a solo planner or working with freelancers on wedding day, you become that person. You go to every vendor, confirm their checklist, and make sure nothing is missed.

And here's a tip most people don't do but absolutely should: Get at least 2–3 contact numbers from every vendor team.

You might be dealing with the business owner when booking, but on event day, it's usually the workers and on-ground managers who are handling the setup. And most of the time? The owner doesn't even come.

So for example, if you're working with a sound and light vendor, know this clearly:

- Who's handling sound?
- Who's handling light?
- Who's the one managing the full team on-site?

This clarity makes coordination much easier, especially under pressure.

The Timeline Is Your Lifeline. But It Can't Run Itself.

The first thing every planner must do before the wedding day, no matter how big or small the scale, is create a detailed timeline.

I'm not talking about just a ceremony-to-reception layout. I mean a comprehensive schedule that outlines:

- Every event
- Every activity

- Every performer, vendor, guest movement, entry, and exit

That timeline is only useful if you have people executing it.

Which brings me to a very important role: the **Backstage Manager**.

The Backstage Manager

Especially for events like the *Sangeet*, you need someone backstage managing:

- Family performances
- Artist entries
- Props
- Timing

A backstage manager ensures the flow doesn't break. They coordinate between the family and the performers, and handle all those little moments where people ask: Who's next? Are we ready? Is the groom's cousin mic'd up?

If you don't have someone managing that, you'll start seeing delays, and missteps.

But What If You're Just Starting Out?

Honestly, not every planner has a big team. When you're starting out, you are the showrunner.

You'll have to handle 80% of the load yourself. You might bring in two or three freelancers. That's fine. But you still have to assign responsibilities smartly. You have to decide who's handling family coordination, who's with the vendors, and who's running point on the timeline.

The day you start growing, when your company can hire full-time staff, that's when you start building departmental roles. But until then, your structure is only as strong as your ability to plan and delegate.

Yes, It Also Comes Down to Budget

The kind of team you bring in depends entirely on what the client is willing to pay for.

If it's a small wedding and the family is hands-on, managing guests, pickups, and food on their own, your job is easier. But when the family expects you to handle everything (welcome dancers, themed entries, coconut counters, logistics, photo ops, *haldi, mehendi, sangeet,* wedding) then you need to price accordingly.

You need to bring in experienced freelancers. And yes, you need to charge for it.

Because otherwise, you'll be doing everything at the same time.

And if you try to do it all yourself, you won't sleep, and even that will not be enough to save the wedding.

You'll wear every hat when you start. But don't wear it for too long. The moment you can delegate with trust, do it. A planner who's rested, present, and focused on the big picture is the one who actually delivers a great wedding.

How Many Managers Do You Really Need? (And What They Actually Cost)

One of the most common questions young planners ask me is: "How do you decide how many managers are needed for a wedding?"

The answer depends on a few factors like budget, scale, number of venues, artist lineups, and the complexity of the flow. But if you're asking for a minimum number then you need at least two. Always. These managers will save you the kind of headaches like a cousin who went missing before her performance.

Oh, I haven't shared this story yet. Have I? Here it is...

The Bride's Cousin Went Missing. So We Rewrote the Show.

This is why I keep saying timelines are sacred. You don't follow them, things start tumbling one by one. And when they do, you need to know how to reset without making a big noise about it.

We had a wedding. And at this one, there was a planned dance performance by the bride and her cousin. It was supposed to happen sharp at 9 PM. Everyone was seated, the music team was ready, lighting cues were in place.

Now the cousin... she disappeared.

Turns out, she had decided she didn't like her makeup. So she wiped it all off. Asked the makeup artist to redo it. Put her phone on charge and just went off-grid.

In the middle of this, she also decided she needed to look fresh. So she went and took a one-and-a-half-hour nap. I'm not making this up.

And this wasn't panic from our side. We were ready. But now, we had no performer & the bride was anxious. So I walked up to her quietly and said,

"Relax. You don't need to perform now. Just sit, smile, cheer loudly, we'll do it at the end."

She nodded. Trusted me and stayed calm.

We called the makeup artist, she said,

"Sir, we finished her makeup exactly the way she told us. Then she said she didn't like it and asked to remove it again."

Eventually, the girl said,

"Just do whatever. I leave it to you."

By the time she landed at the venue, it was 10 PM. The DJ had already started at 9:45. We had permission to play music till 10:30.

Then, just before the DJ's final set, I saw the bride look at me again. I gave her the hand signal. *"All good."*

Now what do you do? We pushed the performance to the end. At 10:20 pm, we announced the "surprise performance."

Now this is where I got a little creative.

I had already called the choreographer and said,

"Let's change the flow. Don't just do a dance. It won't sell as an ending act. So, make it a thing."

Then I had told the choreographer to teach a simple step, and get everyone involved.

We turned it into a full-stage crowd moment. So we had the cousin pull the groom up on stage mid-performance. The groom was a skilled dancer.

Then I pulled the groom aside and said,

"You're going down on one knee. Use her old ring. Propose again. Right here."

We timed it right at the end of the group dance. The groom went down, proposed. People went crazy.

Everyone thought it was part of the plan. Nobody knew this whole thing was damage control.

Honestly, I've done so many of these on-the-spot saves. It's become muscle memory. Because I was a choreographer before I was a planner. It's not that things go wrong. It's what you do when they do.

Clear Com & Real-Time Coordination

Yes, many venues now have walkie-talkies or integrated communication systems. On large-scale weddings, Clear-Com headsets (or any good full-duplex wireless system) become your command center. And if your client hasn't budgeted for it, add it yourself. Trust me, the difference in execution quality and your blood pressure is worth every rupee.

It is the event manager's responsibility to provide a Clear Com set to key members with whom real time coordination is needed throughout the event. Whether it's phone, walkie-talkie, or verbal, someone needs to be following up at all times.

This way, you're not disturbing every department with every message. You talk only to whom you need, exactly when you need.

Guest Experience: From Arrival to Ceremony

If it's a destination wedding or guests are arriving from out of town, then guest flow becomes your next major responsibility.

We usually keep itinerary printouts in guest rooms. It gives them simple schedules with event times, locations, and transport details. But don't assume guests will read them.

You still need a team (or assigned people) to:

- **Guide guests to the venue**

- **Answer questions about timing and seating**
- **Help with movement between events**

In bigger-budget weddings, we assign ushers or guest assistants. In mid-budget weddings, guests manage on their own, and we keep a few people in visible places to help if needed.

Both approaches are fine, but you have to plan accordingly and document both in the SOP.

Essentials for the Bride & Groom: Usually Family-Handled

There's a short list of items that are critical for the bride and groom, and these are almost always managed by the family or close relatives. But that doesn't mean the planner ignores them; you still verify they're ready.

Here's what needs to be packed and prepped:

- Wedding attire
- Footwear
- Accessories (*bangles, dupattas, pagdis, etc.*)
- Rings
- Marriage license and documents
- Other personal items (perfume, safety pins, tissues, etc.)

Each item should be assigned to a family member ahead of time, and ideally, packed into function-wise kits. Don't wait until the morning of the wedding to realise the groom's *jootis* are in a suitcase that went to the other hotel.

Essentials for the Event Manager: Pack Your Outfit. And Then Actually Change Into It.

Now technically, you should pack your own clothes for the wedding, right? Let me tell you, I'm the worst person to talk about this.

If my wife reads this in the book, I'm finished.

She always complains: "You wear the same clothes for two days and land up at the function looking like you came from a warehouse."

And it's true. I don't get time to sleep, where will I get time to change? That adrenaline on wedding days is insane. I'm jumping between four setups and ten vendors.

So my go-to is track pants and a t-shirt. That's my wedding uniform. My wife packs me proper clothes. I pack track pants. And I end up wearing the same ones for two days straight.

She even packs two separate t-shirts for morning and evening. I still wear the same one.

She has told my driver-executive-assistant, who happens to be my childhood friend:

"Don't let him step out until he changes."

And this guy took it personally. He now walks into my room before every event, with kurta in hand, and a serious face. I can't argue. He's seen me since I was 6.

And honestly, it feels good after the change. You feel a little more switched on, people take you more seriously, and your wife doesn't give you *that* look later.

So yeah, fellow planners, pack your clothes. But more importantly, wear them. Otherwise, your assistant will drag you into the washroom and hand you the kurta himself.

Step One: Get the Right Numbers. Not Just the Owner's.

Your job isn't done when you've locked the vendor.
It's done when you've got:

- The owner's number
- The on-ground contact's number (usually the engineer or crew lead)
- Both listed on your timeline sheet

For example, if you're booking a sound vendor, your sheet should show:

- **Vendor Contact**: Owner (handles commercial discussions)
- **Engineer Contact**: Sound technician (handles real execution on-site)

Most owners don't show up at the venue. The engineers, the structure team, the crew, they're the ones who show up and need your coordination.

And yes, we always put these numbers in the master timeline sheet, so anyone in the team can call the right person without hunting.

These numbers are also added to the WhatsApp group, but they must live in the sheet. It's more structured and faster to reference under pressure.

Step Two: Be There When Setup Begins (Or Before)

Don't "arrive early." That's not enough. Arrive earlier than early. You need to be at the venue before the vendors start unloading.

You've already done the recce. You know exactly where things go. You're the one who will guide the teams as they arrive.

Don't leave it to chance. If you show up late, you'll walk in and find setups going in the wrong directions, fabric being draped over the wrong truss, and a pile of confusion you could've avoided.

Step Three: Never Assume the Crew Knows What the Owner Saw

Here's what happens all the time. The vendor owner comes to the recce. He sees the space, discusses placements, and agrees on everything.

But on the wedding day, he doesn't show up. He sends his boys. And 90% of the time, they've got no clue what was agreed. So the first thing you do when a vendor team arrives is you ask:

"Do you know your placements? Do you know which area you're setting up? What goes where?"

If they say no, don't panic. Just walk them through the site again.

If they say yes, great. Still walk them through the site again.

Show them exactly:

- What's going where
- Where the entrance setups are
- Where the truss is going
- Where the floral wall is being placed
- Which stage corner needs which prop

At the end of the day, when something's missing or misplaced, no one's going to call the sound guy, the floral guy, or the truss team. They're going to look for the planner. And that planner is you.

It takes five minutes to verify. And it saves you five hours of fixing.

Family Photos: Where's the Cousin? Probably in the Parking Lot.

Photos are scheduled. Lights are ready. The photographer is shouting, but one cousin is missing. Where is he?

He's in the parking lot, having a drink. When the venue doesn't have a bar, the uncles and other guests figure out their own plan outside.

So here's what I do and what you can do too. Assign a manager to coordinate the wedding party and have one family member act as your internal point of contact. That person helps you get everyone in place for photos, rituals, and entries. Because without them, you will be chasing down drunk uncles instead of running a timeline.

The Alcohol Question: It Will Come Up

Somebody from the family will come up and whisper: *"Bhai, kuch jugaad ho sakta hai kya?"*

Sometimes they want to sneak in bottles. Sometimes they want to set up their own bar at a non-licensed venue. Sometimes they just want you to "handle it quietly."

What should you do? Here's what I do: 90% of the time, I say no.

And if I ever say yes, I don't say it myself. I tell my team to say yes, but with a clause. I tell them:

"If you're saying yes, you're supposed to tell them they are responsible. My company name doesn't get involved."

On the business side, when clients need bar setups or liquor handling, I hand it over to my VP, corporate side. He manages that vertical. One time, he made Rupees 2 lakhs from a single event, just managing the bar side. Fair deal.

Licenses: What You Need to Know

If you're working in a five-star hotel, they already have a liquor license. So no problem there. The hotel serves, you stay out.

But if it's a standalone venue or a private farmhouse, you need a one-day liquor license from the Excise Department. That's the minimum. No license, no bar. Simple as that.

Every Family Has Secrets. You'll Be Dragged into Them Anyway.

We've had situations where staff have been paid extra for keeping secrets and handling sensitive logistics.

Like:

"Make sure she checks in without anyone noticing."

"Don't put us on the same floor as that side of the family."

We've sneaked in the cousin's boyfriends and girlfriends without anyone noticing. You'll be asked to do it quietly. You'll see the groom cheating and the bride cheating. You'll see ugly matters. You'll be pulled in, even if you try to stay neutral.

The *Mamas*, the *Mahira*, and the Budget Battle

Where there's bad, there's also good. You'll likely see some heartwarming bonds, too. There was this one wedding where two *mamas* were supposed to jointly host the *mahira*. One *mama* wanted to go all out with a grand setup. The other didn't, as he had issues with the budget.

Eventually, one of them came to us and said...

"Do something flashy with my budget. Then just collect a chiller amount from his side. Don't tell him how much I actually spent."

He literally asked us to take money from both sides but make it look equal.

We made a grand setup and told the *mama* with less budget that we had some stock in the godown, so we did the best we could with it.

No matter how well you plan, the drama will come. And most of the time, it's about people, their egos, their expectations, and their secrets. Your job isn't to solve everything. But you do need to navigate it without making a mess. And sometimes, that's the real event management.

The new kids entering the industry walk in wide-eyed and are flabbergasted by what they see. And I tell them: *"Welcome to weddings, beta."*

Have a Backup Plan. Always.

Take the bride-and-cousin story we discussed earlier, that's one kind of backup situation.

Then there are physical backups. Like weather, equipment, and last-minute regulations.

When you're working in cities where the weather flips without warning, you must plan for both:

- **Plan A**: your dream setup
- **Plan B**: your damage control setup

Not just mentally though. Plan B must have real structure. That means covering your venue if you're expecting rain, re-routing movement, and protecting the experience.

What is a German Tent? And Why You Should Know It

A German tent is something every planner should learn early.

It is like a large house-shaped truss structure that's:

- Waterproof
- Fireproof
- Available in white or transparent roofing
- Strong enough to protect a full-scale outdoor event

Transparent ones look beautiful, and you get a full view of the sky. But if you want something functional that doesn't show dirt or weather stains, go with white.

You'll also come across dome-shaped structures and other advanced roofing systems. Those come with experience. But a German tent is easy to learn and use. In fact, I will say, never plan an open-air event in dicey weather without having it on standby.

Earlier, people used to set up full superstructures with tin sheets or fabric. Now, German tents are industry standard.

Hidden Risks: Laws, Licenses & Local Government Twists

Unexpected issues aren't always about the weather. Sometimes they're legal. And you won't see it coming.

Take what happened in Bangalore around 2012–13. At one point, dancing was not allowed inside clubs.

Yes, seriously.

The government suddenly announced that to allow dancing, you needed a separate license. Some issues with the excise policy or venue classification. Today it sounds odd, but at one time, this was a law. You couldn't even get up and have a small celebration in the club.

So yes, these things happen. Be aware, plan, and always discuss with the vendors. The only thing worse than not having a Plan B... is pretending you don't need one.

Vendor Being Lazy? Handle It Like This.

See, when you're just starting out, don't act like you know everything.

Let the vendor speak. Ask them, *"Yeh kaise hoga?"*

Let them explain. Then if you've got something better in mind, suggest it.

Not with attitude; just... float the idea.

But sometimes, vendors get lazy. They'll say, *"Nahi ho paayega,"* just because they don't feel like doing it. Now, if you know it can be done, you've seen it before, you're confident, then stand your ground.

There have been times I had to be so rigid with vendors that I told them they have to deliver properly, otherwise the payment will be put on hold.

But only when you know your stuff. You can't bluff your way through that. You need to be sure it works.

- **Stick to the Timeline:**
  - Follow the detailed wedding day timeline closely to ensure everything runs smoothly and on time.
  - Designate a person (wedding planner or coordinator) to oversee the schedule and keep events on track.
- **Communicate with Vendors:**
  - Maintain open lines of communication with all vendors throughout the day to ensure they are on schedule and addressing any needs.
  - Have contact information for all vendors readily available.
- **Monitor Setup:**
  - Arrive early at the venue to oversee the setup and ensure all decor, seating, and equipment are arranged according to the plan.
  - Verify that all areas, including the ceremony site, reception area, and photo locations, are prepared.
- **Coordinate with the Wedding Party:**
  - Keep the bridal party informed of the schedule and any changes.
  - Ensure the wedding party is ready on time for photos, the ceremony, and other key moments.
- **Guest Management:**
  - Ensure guests are informed and guided throughout the day, from arrival to the ceremony to the reception.
  - Arrange for ushers or coordinators to assist with seating and any guest inquiries.

| 27 |

Handling Unexpected Issues

When Things Go Wrong (Because They Will)

Let's not sugarcoat it. Something always goes off-script. The question is: how do you respond when it does?

It's easy to say, "Stay calm. Don't react emotionally. Don't blame." But yes, have a backup plan ready. This is where you need to be a bit of a *jugaadu.*

You can't plan for everything, but you can definitely:

- **Stay Calm and Adaptable:**
    - Remain calm and composed when unexpected issues arise. Quick thinking and a positive attitude can help resolve problems efficiently.
- **Have a Backup Plan:**
    - Prepare contingency plans for potential issues such as bad weather, vendor cancellations, or equipment failures.
    - Ensure alternative options are readily available and feasible.
- **Utilize the Emergency Kit:**
    - Use the emergency kit for quick fixes to attire, makeup, or minor injuries.
- **Delegate Problem-Solving:**

    - Rely on your team (wedding planner, coordinator, or trusted individuals) to handle minor issues, allowing you to focus on enjoying the day.
- **Vendor Support:**
    - Lean on your vendors for support; they have experience handling various situations and can often provide quick solutions.
- **Communication:**
    - Keep lines of communication open with the wedding party, vendors, and key guests to quickly address and resolve any issues.
- **Focus on the Big Picture:**
    - Remember that the wedding is about celebrating love and commitment. Small hiccups are inevitable, but they shouldn't overshadow the joy of the day.

When the Cake Fell Apart... Literally

We were doing an engagement event in Tumkur. Beautiful setup. We'd ordered a proper 3-tier cake. Some kids went in there to change clothes and somehow, the cake got damaged.

But to be honest, I still think it wasn't the kids' fault. I think it was the driver's fault.

Because the way he sped his car while carrying that cake...Boss, it's a 3-tier cake. Not a parcel from Swiggy. The cake was gone.

And at the last minute, we had to use the anniversary cake that was meant for the bride's parents for cake cutting.

Now, let me explain why this happened.

Usually, when you work with freelancers, they come to the venue themselves, set up the cake properly, and handle everything.

But bakeries don't do that. We'd ordered from a boutique cake outlet. They had amazing products, great prices, but no on-site service, of course.

When I compared:

- **Boutique vendor:** Rupees 14,000 total
- **Freelancer baker's quote:** Rupees 24,000 + transport + taxes + setup

And this was Tumkur, about 70 km away.

So yes, I saved Rupees 10,000, but it wasn't worth the mess that happened.

The Next Morning: A Sweet Recovery

The next morning, I had a fresh cake made and sent to her house. She called me and said,

"Your wife must be really happy with you. You know how to win hearts."

I laughed and said,

"You clearly haven't met my wife. She's banned surprises."

No planner's wife is happy with last-minute ideas.

What Went Wrong with the Lift

This happened recently. My team was coordinating the logistics for a decor setup. There was a lift at the hotel. We asked the property for dimensions, and the response we got was 'a car can go in.'

Now when you hear that, you assume it's a big service lift. But no one from my team went to physically check the size.

The actual lift was 16 by 8.5 feet. And our panels were 20 by 10-foot iron panels. These are solid structures. You can't bend them, tilt them, or fold them. Your only options are:

1. Cut and weld them back again (not ideal on site).
2. Rebuild the same panel from smaller wooden pieces (what we call reapers) and assemble on-site.

So I told them to bring extra wooden reapers, attach them from the top, and make the frame there.

Could it have been avoided? 100%. But it wasn't because the lift wasn't physically measured.

Another Planner, Same Mistake

Something similar happened recently with another wedding planner who was renting panels from us. She said she had an event at the Taj, but didn't mention which Taj. She also didn't ask about service lift dimensions or staircase access.

We sent the full-sized panels as requested. Neither the lift nor the stairs could accommodate the panels.

She messaged at 2:00 AM, in a panic, asking if there was any solution. When I saw the message the next morning, I told her the same thing: "You should have cut the panel down and assembled it in parts."

This is what she said, "I know, I should have spoken to you first."

Now, what is a reaper? A reaper is essentially a wooden beam or frame strip used to assemble structures when you can't bring full panels in. In Hindi, we call it *lakdi.*

You can use reapers to reconstruct any large panel on-site. It's not ideal, but it's the *jugaad* that saves you when you don't have time to weld iron or when you're working with tricky access points.

People have different names for it. Some call it framing, some call it battening. Doesn't matter. What matters is knowing when to switch from iron to reaper.

MODULE 9

CLIENT & VENDOR COMMUNICATION

"In weddings, what's not written is forgotten, and what's not followed up becomes chaos. Clarity, documentation, and timing aren't just good habits; they're your insurance policy against disaster."

- ***Zubair Abdul Waheed***

| 28 |

Clear Communication & Conflict Resolution

Keep Communication Simple, Clear, and Documented

Always use clear, straightforward language when you speak with clients. After every meeting, whether it's a casual call or a big discussion, send a follow-up.

Either:

- A MOM (Minutes of Meeting),
- Or send a simple WhatsApp message that says: "This is what we discussed. This is what we agreed on."

Why? Because during the planning phase, you'll throw 100 ideas at them. But when the budgets are finalised, many of those ideas get cut.

Fast forward to the wedding day, suddenly the client remembers something you spoke about in Week 1.

And they go:

"You didn't do that."

"We had discussed this."

And I say,

"Jo excel sheet mein likha hai, wahi hoga na."

There was this one client. He tells me,

"We had selected this earlier, why didn't it get delivered?"

I told him, "If I go to your gold shop and see 100 things, but I only buy the one I paid for, right? Not the first 100 things I had touched."
He went, "That's different, this is a wedding."
I said, "It's the same thing. It's still business."

After that wedding, we decided no more verbal nonsense. We started doing contracts.

Do We Contract Everyone? No. Just the Risky Ones.

I don't do contracts with every client. But if it's a *Marwari family*, or a *Muslim family*...yes, I do a contract.

Because with both, you never know when they'll flip. They'll push you to the limit and want everything at the original price, and not a rupee more.

And when that happens, I put my foot down. I've even switched off lights once to make a point.

If They Want Extras, They Pay for Extras

If they want something extra, they raise a request. We upload a picture, send the quote. If they approve, we do it. If they don't, we leave it.

Because otherwise they keep saying: "Just do it, we'll see later."

Then later becomes *"Chhod na yaar, extra tha hi kya."*

And suddenly you're Rupees 12 lakhs over budget. I've had this happen. One client just shut the laptop and said,

"Take what you have. I'm not paying more."

I told him straight:

"Sir, aap hotel nahi chhod paayenge." (Sir, you won't be able to leave the hotel premises.)

He was shocked. I said,

"I have all the permissions filed with the police. You can't check out until this is settled."

He closed it at Rupees 10 lakhs. Sometimes you need to get firm. Very firm.

If It's Not in Writing, It Doesn't Exist. And if it's in writing, nobody can argue. Simple.

Keep the Channel Open (Even for Things You Dread Saying)

Always keep communication open. Encourage your vendors and clients to ask questions. Even if there is an update that might disappoint people, share it. Don't block it just because you're worried they'll say no to paying extra or be disappointed.

In fact, I would say, bring it up early. A lot of planners try to avoid awkward topics. They assume rejection or the worst outcome. They think,

"Yeh mana kar denge. Chhodo."

But when you do raise it, the client might surprise you. There have been so many cases where clients insisted on something in a meeting, but when it didn't work out, they were totally okay with an alternative. You HAVE to be honest.

If you try to cover it up or give excuses, they might stay quiet in the moment... but they'll bring it up later. Usually, when you're asking for final payment.

When Guests Start Complaining & Things Get Heated...

There's a popular line from a Hindi song *"Kuch toh log kahenge, logon ka kaam hai kehna". (People will talk, it's their job to talk.)*

The same happens at a wedding. Guests are there to complain, nitpick, and remark negatively even on the perfect things. When a guest complains about the food, the rooms, the weather, or the hotel, don't jump to defend anyone.

Especially not the hotel.

If you side with the hotel, the family feels you're taking the hotel's side.

Instead, be neutral. Never take it on yourself. Frame your response as "this is what THE HOTEL people object with". For example: "Sir, the hotel has a concern. Let me check how we can handle it without disrupting anything."

Validate the client's concern, but also keep the venue relationship intact.

Listen Actively, Solve Practically

Ask questions.
Understand what the client or vendor really wants.
Then figure out what's actually possible.

And always steer conversations toward the outcome. Not the drama.

I always ask:

"What's the final result you're hoping for?"
"What are the options we're looking at?"
"What does the client want, and what's the venue willing to allow?"

Once you get both sides, you can offer a solution that works for everyone.

The *Mandap* in the Pool

We had a bride who wanted the *Mandap* on the pool. And initially, the hotel manager agreed. So we planned accordingly. Then, out of nowhere, the hotel said that we'll have to pay
Rupees 1 lakh extra to the hotel just to use the pool for building a *Mandap* on the pool.

We were all flustered. 1 lakh is not a small miscellaneous cost that you can add to the budget. So we asked the hotel the rationale behind this added cost. What they said made sense. Once you use the pool, they have to drain and refill the water. That costs money. I called a few hotelier friends of mine and enquired. They all agreed that this is the standard protocol and rate. Fair, so we told the client upfront.

The client asked me why THEY should give 1 lakh more in the budget for this.

I told him honestly,

"If it is costing us 1 lakh more, then of course, we'll have to ask you, right? All hotels do this. If the water gets used, they'll charge for it."

Eventually, the bride agreed on having the *Mandap* built in the garden beside the pool. Eventually we still had a pool in the backdrop of the photos, it was just that the *Mandap* was not in the pool.

We shifted it. And thank God we did because it rained the entire time.

Flexibility Solves More Than Planning Ever Can

And even though it rained during setup, we had already covered the ceiling with a German tent. The flooring was a bit wet, but nothing major. By the time the ceremony began, the rain had stopped. *Mandap* stayed dry and photos came out great.

Everyone was happy.

I wasn't even there. I was packing up another wedding. But the system worked. Because the client was informed, the venue was prepared, and we'd already built Plan B. See how everything is coming together?

Conflicts Don't Just Come from Logistics

It's not always about sound, decor, or timelines.

Sometimes it's this...Who got more sweets to distribute? Who got the better entry setup? Why did the groom's mom get her way and the bride didn't?

These sound small. But in a wedding setup, these become major flashpoints.

A lot of times, we solve something and then move on. You've resolved a seating issue, but then you forget to follow through. And then what happens? That same issue resurfaces on the wedding day.

So I always tell my team:

"Any conflict we resolved, follow up, execute, and update the people involved in the resolution. Don't leave it hanging."

Do it even when the family says "It's fine." Sometimes people agree just to avoid drama, especially the bride's side. They'll say yes under pressure, but you can tell they're not happy.

Even after resolving them, someone might change their mind 30 minutes later and reignite the whole thing.

One Guy. There's Always One Guy.

We create a detailed timeline for every wedding, down to the hour, and then we hand it over to everyone: the team, vendors and family of the bride and groom.

Because often, the bride or groom doesn't come to the venue during setup. It's the cousins, the friends, the brother-in-law's younger brother. And when they arrive, they start pointing fingers, trying to act important.

We've seen people, especially at high-profile weddings, who come just to look for mistakes. They want to "impress" the main client by catching errors.

At one wedding, we finished setting up the *Nikah* stage. It looked perfect. But this one gentleman, who's apparently a stage designer himself, walks in and says,

"This 3D layer didn't come out well."

He walked right in, ignored the full decor, and pointed out one corner in the backdrop that was not meant to draw attention of people.

Then he went and told the client. Now, the thing is, I had already warned the client that something like this would happen. I know this client well. So when I met him, I said,

"Sir, someone told me you got feedback on the *Nikah* decor?"

He laughed and said,

"Yeah, so-and-so came and said the same thing. I told him to relax."

Trust me, some people's entire personality is built around finding faults (even where there aren't any). Beware of these people. You can spot them saying *"Yeh theek nahi laga. Woh better ho sakta tha."*

You can't change them. You just need to know how to spot them, handle them politely, and then... ignore them.

Until you've seen what can go wrong, you don't realise how small things like a missed tech rider or an unclear instruction can snowball into Rupees 7-lakh-sized problems.

When to Meet, When to Update, and What to Ask After It's All Done

People often ask me: *"Zubair bhai, how do you decide when to have meetings? How often do you update the client?"*

Simple answer: *When it's needed.*

Don't Keep Buzzing the Client Like a Notification

If you keep giving updates every few hours, clients will start chasing you for updates. Then the pressure shifts, you'll waste time answering questions instead of executing.

Best thing is to keep them informed, but keep it tight.

Whenever something important comes up, like a final approval or something that needs a decision, pick up the phone and call.

"This is needed, and here's why."

You don't wait for them to ask. You tell them before it becomes a problem.

4-Hour Meeting. Full Wedding Done.

When we did Shreyas Gopal's wedding (the IPL cricketer), I only had one meeting day. It ran for 4 hours to be precise. That's it.

After that, there were no daily calls. We had a WhatsApp group, we'd drop updates, and they'd trust us. And that trust gives you full freedom to work properly.

When Do You Actually Need a Meeting?

Only when:

- You need approvals
- Something big has changed
- The client is confused or stuck

Otherwise, there's no need. They've hired you so they don't have to micro-manage.

MODULE 10

AFTER THE WEDDING

*"Final payments aren't receipts, they're report cards. How you settle accounts determines who shows up for your next wedding."***-Zubair Abdul Waheed**

| 29 |

Post-Wedding Wrap-Up

Finalising Vendor Payments and Tips

Most people assume this is just a closing formality. *Event khatam, paisa dedo,* done.

Well, not quite. This bit is just as important as the planning or setup. Go over every agreement. Cross-check what's pending. If someone worked overtime, acknowledge it, not just with a pat on the back. Give a bonus where it's due. Thank the ones who were on their feet for 14 hours straight.

People remember how you treated them and made them feel. And when you close cleanly, respectfully, and generously, they don't forget. And they come back ready to give you 200% next time.

After the Wedding, Don't Ask "How Was It?"

After the wedding is over, don't ask: "How was the experience?"

You won't get real feedback. Instead, you should ask: "What could we have done better?"

It shows you're serious about improving.

And you'll always get something useful from that, even if the event went great. Sometimes they'll just say one small thing. But that small thing can be the difference between a great event and an unforgettable event.

That's how I've improved over the years.

Reflecting on the Event and Areas for Improvement

After every event, I sit down with my team. We ask ourselves:

- What went right?
- What went wrong?
- What slipped through?
- What did we manage to save last minute?

Even after 7000+ events, we still do this. Because the moment you think there's nothing to improve, the industry will kick you out.

Whether it's a cousin who vanished during the *baraat* dance or a vendor who delivered late, you note it. Learn from it. And next time, you fix it before it becomes an issue.

| 30 |

Trends, Mentors, & Lifelong Learning

One thing people don't talk about enough in the wedding industry is learning. This isn't a job where you do 10 weddings and you know it all. There's always something new happening, new trends, new technology, new problems.

So what do you do? You keep learning.

Stay Updated or Stay Behind

If you're in this industry, you need to follow the right people... Instagram, LinkedIn, wedding forums, Pinterest moodboards; whatever gives you a sense of what's coming up.

But even more important is to attend industry conventions.

ICWF, EMMA, or any other platform where seniors are sharing, you should show up.

That's where you see what your seniors are doing. That's where you learn from the best, from the real experiences of what works and what doesn't.

Learn From People Who've Done It

I recently reached out to Ritu Raj Khanna, the CEO of Q Events and the OG of the luxury wedding scene. He is one of the top wedding decorators in the country.

I sat with him for a proper 90-minute session and asked all the questions I had. Questions like how to manage godowns and handling back-end ops. Stuff I was struggling with.

And I learnt more in those 90 minutes than in weeks of trying to figure it out on my own.

You're Only As Good As What You Keep Learning

Right now, I'm learning too. I take sessions from people like Paritosh, sit in on panels, ask questions, read global trend reports. You stay at the top by always staying a student.

And if you're willing to keep learning, there's space for you at the top too.

| 31 |

How the Industry (and I) Changed

When I started out, it was a completely different world. There was no social media, no Pinterest, no AI. You learnt by doing and failing. Technically, you still learn by doing and failing but now there's more to events and there's more tools you can take help from.

Back in the day, if we needed a custom design, we'd sit down with a hand sketch artist.

You'd explain the vision. He'd draw it, by hand, on a piece of paper with a pencil. We'd take that rough sketch to the client and say:

"This is what your decor might look like."

Clients didn't have digital references, or moodboards. They looked at printed photos from our old events, stored in a big album.

That was our "portfolio."

Now? One Prompt Gives You 10 Visuals.

Recently, a client came to us and said:

"I want an abstract Krishna theme."

Honestly, even he didn't know what he meant. We tried Pinterest. It didn't work. We searched everywhere. Nothing matched.

So I turned to ChatGPT. I gave it prompts like:

"Abstract Krishna wedding theme."

"Modern Krishna decor style."

It gave me a few visual ideas. From there, I created a proper deck, showed it to the client.

You won't believe this, but he loved it! That's how digitisation has changed events industry for many of us.

Then vs Now: Industry Culture

Earlier, when I entered the industry, everyone saw you as competition.

No one would share vendor contacts. They'd even quote absurd rates just to throw you off. There were no associations or real communities to support you. People were doing their own thing.

Now, it's better. We've got industry associations, WhatsApp groups, conventions. Even though we're competitors, we collaborate. We share vendors. We share knowledge.

Yes, there are still people who play dirty, but it's much less now.

In fact, in today's day and age, your biggest competitor might be your best friend in a crisis.

Seriously. If I'm stuck last minute and I need a vendor I can't find, I'll call one of my competitors. And they'll say:

"Yeh vendor ke paas hai, check kar le."

That's a real-time support that the events industry never had back in those days.

Just a few weeks ago, we had a green velvet cloth shortage. All our vendors were out of stock. So I put a message in our Bangalore Wedding Planners WhatsApp group (filled with my direct competitors).

Within minutes, I had 3–4 new numbers of vendors. Not only was my problem solved, but also my network of vendors expanded with just 1 message in a group.

So yes, **the person you're competing with today might save your event tomorrow.**

| 32 |

Final Thoughts to Carry with You

As you embark on your journey as wedding planners, remember that you are stepping into a role that is both immensely rewarding and profoundly impactful. You will have the privilege of helping couples create one of the most memorable days of their lives. Here are a few final thoughts to carry with you:

Passion and Commitment:

Let your passion for weddings and events drive you. Your commitment to excellence will be reflected in the joy and satisfaction of your clients.

Continuous Learning:

The wedding industry is ever-evolving. Stay curious, keep learning, and adapt to new trends and technologies. Your willingness to grow will keep you at the forefront of the industry.

Empathy and Understanding:

Always approach your clients with empathy and understanding. Each couple's story is unique, and your ability to listen and connect will set you apart.

Creativity and Innovation:

Embrace your creativity and strive to bring fresh ideas to every wedding you plan. Innovation and personal touches will make each event truly special.

Professionalism and Reliability:

Build a reputation for professionalism and reliability. Your clients will trust and rely on you during some of the most important moments of their lives.

Enjoy the Journey:

Finally, enjoy the journey. The world of wedding planning is filled with beautiful moments, challenges, and opportunities to create lasting memories. Embrace each experience and take pride in the happiness you help create.

- Congratulations on completing this course. Your journey as a wedding planner is just beginning, and the future holds endless possibilities. Go forth with confidence, creativity, and a heart full of enthusiasm. The weddings you plan will undoubtedly be a testament to your talent and dedication.
- Best of luck to you all, and may your careers be as beautiful and fulfilling as the weddings you create.

| 33 |

Find Me Here

Instagram

https://www.instagram.com/zubairzzeeh

@ZUBAIRZZEEH

LinkedIn

https://www.linkedin.com/in/zubair-abdul-waheed-16aa6333/

COMPANY- ZZEEH PRODUCTIONS PVT LTD

https://www.zzeehweddings.com

9 789334 355772

Printed at Repro India Ltd.